CHILD 6150

Dedicated to all those who have been abandoned by their families

and thrown into the pits of hell;

To all those who have lost their life in a system based on

corruption, exploitation and torture;

To all those whom society had deemed worthless…

1

Written By

Danny Lee Amos

Table of Contents

*I've been in numerous other prisons than those listed

Foreward

Although I continue to suffer from a lifetime of punishment filled with nightmares of torture and abuse, I pray that my ordeal will touch the hearts of those who are in the position to bring about change, and I hope that this book will advocate for the reform of our penal system. Abandoned by my family at the age of 10, I have spent the last 50 years of my life in confinement. During those years I have been incarcerated within facilities through the entire United States, including some of the worst prisons in existence today. This book is not written for anyone to feel sorry for me, it's written to bring light to the issues of our penal system so that no child should ever have to go through what I and so many others were forced to endure.

It's immoral that here in the United States, society would allow the justice system to impose a term of over 50 years on someone who has not committed a crime that would justify such a sentence. While there have been many books written about the injustices and conditions within today's prisons, no book has ever been written from as far back as a child's perspective - until now. But before I begin, I'd like to thank everyone who has worked so hard to bring my life's ordeal to the public eye.

At this point in my life, my only desire is to tell my story to anyone who will listen. I hope to be able to help someone through whatever struggle they may be dealing with. If I'm able to help one single person avoid life in the *system*, then I'll know that my existence has been to serve a noble purpose in this world. The juvenile judge's words still resonate in my mind from all of those years ago when he said, "Lock him away for as long as the law will allow." Later on as an adult, the last judge who sentenced me basically followed suite by saying, "Lock him away until he's a senior citizen." Mind you, I've never committed a crime deemed heinous by society, or in the eyes of the law, that would be worthy of imposing such an extensive prison term. My crimes as an adult consisted of survival related charges within the prison system, and numerous escapes from my tormenters. Throughout my years of incarceration, I have come to accept that fact that prison is nothing more than a government run business where the *system* is the boss. I strongly believe that if the system's transgressions against me were brought to light, I would have been freed many years ago.

This is the story of a child who from age 10, was forced to live in confinement all of his life. Lost and unknown to the world, he lives today.

I pray that this book will open up your hearts and minds as you read. I hope that perhaps this story will in some way help parents, the people of society, and those in the appropriate positions to bring forth the changes we need in our Prison System so that no child or human being will ever have to experience the following nightmares in life that I had to endure. I hope this story will cause your mind and heart to question why here in the United States a child could possibly suffer in the hands of prison officials, and be forced to be confined for 50 years in 34 different prisons in some of the worst conditions imaginable without committing a crime that would call for such a punishment.

This is the story of Child No. 6150…

All stories in this book are true. Names, places, and identifying details of certain individuals have been changed in order to protect their anonymity.

Chapter 1

A Day in My Life

It's morning and as I'm sitting in my locked cage, a cell no bigger than a small bathroom, made of concrete and steel, I hear some inmates talking to each other through the vents above the toilets about their families. They're comparing what they once had, to what they will have once they leave prison.

But as I'm listening to them, I also start to hear the abuse being inflicted upon yet another inmate by the guards. The sounds, all too familiar within my own past, alerted me once again to the danger that was present. Up and ready for the worst, I moved quickly to my cell door.

As I pressed my ear up against the bars, I could clearly hear the cries of the young man just four cells down from mine. He was crying out for help as he begged the guards to stop kicking and beating him. By now, other inmates are yelling to the guards to leave the kid alone, and challenging them to come to their own cells if they think they're so tough. The guards, who have always made it a point to let us know how they feel about us, did not hesitate for a second to respond. One guard looked toward an inmate and told him not to worry, he was next, and if anyone else wanted to get in the action all we had to do was let him know. Then the guard asked, "Why do you think society has thrown you animals away?" He answered his own question by saying, "It's because the world is better off without you in it, and that's why we get paid to kill you."

I will never forget how sick my stomach felt as I heard and watched several guards dragging that kid to solitary *(a means of abuse which is now days referred to as "Ad Seg" [Administrative Segregation])* across the concrete floor. Although he was bleeding, some of the guards kept kicking his helpless body, and as he got closer, I could see the fear in his eyes as he looked up at me. It was at that moment that one of the guards looked at me and said, "Amos, you're next. We still haven't had enough of you yet."

Those were terrifying words to hear, especially since at the time I was confined to a solitary cell in what is known as a 'Super Max' facility for stabbing the guard who had broken my hand a few months earlier. Understand this: it doesn't matter to anyone that I was being denied my meal and that in hopes of receiving something to eat, I kept the food trap open with my hand. Nor that the guard, who was training a female officer at the time, obviously wanted to show off and kicked the food trap shut so hard that it broke my hand. It doesn't even matter that after he broke my hand and told me that I was an animal, I was also denied medical treatment for the injuries that he inflicted. As a matter of fact, I was denied any type of medical attention during that entire year I was in solitary confinement. Sadly, the only thing that does matter in prison is that I retaliated against the brutality brought upon me by the guard.

After the guards cleared out, I heard the other inmates talking again through the vents from cell to cell. This time they were talking about how the kid was removed from his cell so that the cellblock officer could conduct a search for contraband. They said that since the guard didn't find anything, he became angry and decided to dump the kid's three-day-old trash on his bed. Rumor had it that when the kid asked the guard why he dumped the trash on his bed, that triggered the beating. The guard's response was that he was no one to question what he did, and that he was going to show him how he ran his house.

Later that day, news from the guards was that the animal hanged himself in solitary. Even though they bragged about the kid killing himself, we all knew that the real reason he was dead was because the guards had beaten him to death.

Although that kid had died many years ago, I must admit that it is a long and lasting memory. The experience was so traumatic that when I recalled the guard saying the words "my house", I was immediately flooded with childhood memories of Leavenworth. While I became nothing more to the state of Missouri than property at an extremely young age, it was at the age of 8 that I started getting into trouble, and by the time I was 10, I had a police record. There were a few years of my life when I was a brother, son and grandson before becoming a number in the system. None of those years were filled with memories of a happy home or childhood, but nonetheless, they're the only ones I have.

Chapter 2

Family

Despite my mother's botched attempt to abort me, I'm the eldest of eight children. I am the product of an Irish and Cherokee Union, and was born in Jefferson City, MO just two days after St. Patty's Day in 1951. Unlike many children born of biracial parents, I was given two distinct names at birth. I was given what I presume to be a somewhat traditional Catholic and Irish name right out of the Bible - Danny, and was also honored by a great tribal member of the Cherokees who gave me the traditional name of *Running Wolf.* Running means "With Greatness" and Wolf means "Warrior Against the Enemy". Ironically enough, this is a name that I was forced to live up to.

I remember living in one house as a child. It was a nice, big house that my father had bought several miles from his mother in a fairly poor, and predominately Spanish and Italian section of Kansas City. I always brought home stray dogs that I felt needed help, but was never able to keep any of them very long, and until my grandmother took me in, schooling was essentially nonexistent.

Although I lived in my father's house with my mother and siblings, her rejection was very apparent to me early in life. The only feeling for me at "home" was that of wretched worthlessness. While my father's absence during most of my life forced me to fend for myself at an early age, it was my mother's (and her boyfriend's) resentment towards me that ultimately pushed me into the streets of

Missouri when I was barely 8 years old. The man who my mother brought into my father's house while he was imprisoned treated her and the other kids well, but he openly hated me - something my mother never had a problem with.

My mother had been living in a geriatric home in Kansas City for years now. Even though I don't think that she'll live long enough to see my release from prison in the year 2015, and despite all the pain and suffering that she has inflicted upon me, I would still like to show my respect as her son just once more before she leaves this earth. Unfortunately, this didn't happen. My mother died on March 25, 2015. 147 days before I was released.

With regards to my father, I can't remember the first time he was locked up, but as far back as I can remember, he spent most of his life in and out of prison. I was the only one who visited him on the weekends. I would go with my grandmother whenever she was able to make the trip to Leavenworth, and every time I saw him, I saw in his face that prison was taking its toll on him.

My father was released from prison over 20 years ago for the last time. Upon his release, he remarried and fathered a couple more kids. Although in bad health and in his forties when he was freed, he managed to start up his own 'legitimate' construction business. Sadly, despite his success, he lived a very hard life. About 14 years ago I escaped from prison, and while a fugitive, I stayed with my father and his new wife in Kansas. His depression and drunk driving eventually caused his painful death, but before he died, I worked beside him for 9 months. During that time, his remorse must've hit him like a sledgehammer because I knew that he remembered many of the devilish acts that he had committed earlier in his life, including the wrongs he did towards me as a child. Despite telling him that I forgave him, a couple of times I came close to taking

13

revenge. I felt that despite my forgiveness, he deserved to be punished for his actions against me and my sister. *He raped her a couple of times and mistreated her terribly.* Ultimately I decided to just let it go, along with the rest of my childhood and adolescent nightmares.

While staying with my dad I took on a different name, assumed a new identity, and essentially took over my father's business. By leading a crime-free life and working hard every day, I had made enough money to get my own place out in the countryside. I owned 9 dogs, and even found a girlfriend who moved in with me. Life was so good that I blocked the fact that I had escaped from a State Penitentiary altogether. As a matter of fact, my false papers looked so authentic that I actually went to the city courthouse to pay for two traffic tickets that I had received.

I remember thinking during my escape from prison that I wasn't going to make it. I had been out in the swamps for a few days praying to God that he allow me to be free, even if just for a short time. I thought, 'God, please let me make it home so that I can have some free time in the real world.' My escape prompted special attention, so the prison had all the authorities out looking for me. While hiding out in the swamps, I stepped on something sharp that had cut my foot open. Despite the pain and severe bleeding, I pressed on. I finally made it out of the state and I knew that God had answered my prayer.

I eventually earned enough money to buy a couple of trucks, and was trying to buy the house that I had been renting in the country. Being out there brought me the freedom and happiness that I have long since desired. I would gladly go to work in the mornings, and eagerly come home in the evenings. Living so far away from people gave me the opportunity to live out some of my dreams, and helped me recognize that although I have been institutionalized for most of my life, I can still lead a *normal* life. Contrary to what the system tried to instill in me for years, I proved that I could function in society as a hard-working, law-abiding citizen.

Unfortunately, the *system* wasn't the only one that wanted me to live in a cage. Believe it or not, it turned out that my own brother and my father's wife had turned me into the authorities. Maybe they were envious of my happiness, maybe they had their sights on my meager assets and would stop at nothing to get them, or maybe they were just wicked people. I guess what they say is true - nobody can hurt you like family.

In any event, I told the judge my story and how I had proven that I'm not a worthless human being, but instead someone who can be a productive member of society if given the opportunity. Unlike my brother (he died in July 2006 of a drug overdose) and my father's wife, I don't envy anyone for what they may have been able to accomplish in life. Much to my surprise, the judge was somewhat lenient in sentencing me. He only added 13 years (he could've added a lot more time than that since it wasn't my first escape) to my existing sentence, which brought my bid in state to 30 years. Incredibly, when my state bid started in 1983, it was for only 7 years. Subsequently, 23 years were added over time for self-defense against convicts and corrupt guards, in addition to the 13 years I was just charged with.

Thinking back on my life at the age of 8, I felt joy knowing that within a few days my paternal grandmother was taking me to visit my father who was confined at the United States Federal Penitentiary in Leavenworth, Kansas for bank robbery. My grandmother, like me, had Cherokee blood running through her body, and she was a beautiful woman full of pride, although very

15

temperamental. She had long, silky-dark hair, typical of a Cherokee, with front teeth laden in gold that would beam through her wonderful smile.

Her words echo in my thoughts still today as if she were speaking to me right now. When we drove to Leavenworth she always said to me, "Danny Lee, you're just like your father, and if you're no good mother doesn't keep you from running the streets till all hours of the night, you're going to end up in the same cell as your father. Do hear me, Running Wolf?"

What my grandmother didn't understand was that to an 8-year-old who was loathed by his mother, the very thought of being loved by someone was so overwhelming that it didn't matter where he got it. As she always said those words to me, my response to her was always that I didn't care because my father needed me with him. *Little did I know back then that my life as I knew it was destined to be over by my 10*th *birthday.*

Leavenworth is a large, long, white building with bars all over the outer walls. There is a big dome that resembled the pictures I saw on TV of the Presidential White House in Washington, DC. As we approached the main compound, my grandmother drove toward a large tower that housed a guard carrying a very large gun. I remember asking my grandmother why the guard carried such a big gun all the time. She told me the reason was because when my father was 8 years old he was a bad boy like me, so now the guard had a machine gun to watch over him and keep him out of trouble. Once we reached the tower, the guard used an intercom to ask my grandmother to state her business. As always she announced that we were there to visit my father, and identified who we were by name. She also referred to my father's Federal ID number so that he could be found within the prison population. *Something that anyone who's not familiar with the correctional system needs to realize is that once you become part of the system, dehumanization plays an essential role in the punishment (A.K.A rehabilitation) process. Upon entering, you are immediately stripped of your 'human' identity and are no longer recognized as a person, but instead as a cataloged item within a human warehouse.* When the guard reiterated the information given by my grandmother, he casually asked her if I was Amos' son, and she responded, "Yes, the other half of him."

On one particular day the tower guard nodded my way and told me that I better be good for my grandmother and do as she told me because I didn't want to end up there like my father. He told me that I wouldn't want to live in 'his house'. Naïvely, I didn't hesitate to tell the tower guard that I wanted to be with my father because he needed me, even if we both had to live at Leavenworth. Dumbfounded by my response, the guard looked back at my grandmother and with a smirk told her that she certainly had her hands full with me!

Once we cleared the checkpoint we proceeded to the main compound and parked in the visitors' lot. As I got out of the car, I saw a dome past a multitude of stairs that lead up to a simple gate constructed of wrought iron bars. I helped my grandmother up the '144 stairs' that lead us past the gate, and into the dome that was filled with loud sounds of prisoners and guards alike. Though I could not understand what they were saying, the guards routinely walked around, addressing the prisoners. Once we made it through the dome, we were led into a room where my grandmother and I were searched by another big guard.

I was at first scared by the whole process, and even asked my grandmother if we had done something wrong. The big guard who was searching us heard what I had asked my grandmother and brazenly said, "Not today son, but if you aren't good, I have a cell here for you. Make sure you ask your father what he thinks of my rooms. Always remember, be a good boy or your Uncle Sam will give you to me, and no one here likes me." Petrified by his words, I froze and wondered if he had been mean to my father. I vaguely felt my grandmother hastily take me by the hand and tell me to "move it" before that nasty man took me with him.

After what seemed to be an eternal wait, my father was finally allowed to join us. We sat in the prison visiting area, and were able to sit with him at a table by ourselves. During this particular visit, my father told me that he would be coming home in a few years and that until he returned, he expected me to be the man of the house. I listened to my father and despite knowing that it was his house, I had to tell him that I couldn't be the man of the house. When he asked me why not, I felt obligated to tell him about mom's boyfriend; the man who mom said was her new husband. I also told him that she had brought him to live at the house with her, and how he had told all of us that 'he was in charge of the house' now. When my father asked me what I meant by 'he's in charge of the house,' I started to tell him everything. I told him about the boyfriend moving into the house a long time ago, and how mom's belly was really big now. Then, I told him how mom had told us that we were going to have another sister or brother, and that since the boyfriend was our father now and in charge, we would have to do what he said.

Although I could see my father was in total shock of what I was telling him, I kept talking. I told him about telling mom that I wasn't going to do anything that man said, because he wasn't in charge of my father's house, and that she told me that if I didn't do what he said, she was going to send me to live with my no good father. I even told him that I had let mom know that he would be coming home soon, and how she cut me right off and told me that he wouldn't be living there again. I also told him that as soon as that man heard what mom and I were talking about, he jumped in and told me that if my father ever came around, he'd shoot him like a dog.

By now I could see that my father was really getting mad, but I kept telling him about the things that were going on in *his* house while he wasn't there. I told him after that man said he was going to shoot my father like a dog, he looked at me and said angrily, "Speaking of dogs, you better get rid of that sorry hound you brought to *my* house before I blow him away as well! I can't feed you mangy kids, let alone a damn dog, and if you don't get rid of him I swear boy I'll shoot him and feed him to you brats!"

I continued to tell my father that I told that man he better not shoot my dog because if he did, my dad would shoot him. That man got so angry he told me he hated me, and I was nothing but a brat. He then told me if I kept messing with him, he'd do to me what he was going to do to my father when he got out, and then he told Mom that I was rotten to the core. He also told Mom that if she didn't get rid of me, he was going to leave her. So mom told him she was going to talk to grandma and if she didn't want me, she was going to turn me over to the state. *What I never did tell my father was how deserted I felt when my mother made it perfectly clear that day that she couldn't care less about me and chose him, and how heartbroken I was from seeing the resentment in her face every time she looked at me.*

By the time I finished telling my father all about mom and her boyfriend he was furious. He looked at my grandmother and asked her if she knew what was going on. He wanted to know about the guy who moved into his house, and who did he think he was,

19

saying all those things to *his son – in his house*! He told grandma that he knew something wasn't right when mom stopped writing him, and that if that man was still in the house he paid for when he got out, or hurt any of his kids, he was going to kill him. He went on to say that he should have left mom when she ran off pregnant with me and found her lying in a St. Louis motel bleeding to death after trying to abort me with a clothes hanger. He said that if he hadn't rushed mom to the hospital, we probably both would've died.

My grandmother looked at my father and said "Ed, you knew a long time ago that she never wanted Danny, and with you in and out of prison and jail all the time, it's no wonder that he's running the streets till all hours of the night and getting into trouble. She doesn't care what happens to him. She only cares about the new man of hers and the other kids, and I'll bet that they'll end up in trouble just like Danny as long as she's with that man, especially now that she's going to have his baby. Danny is living on the streets and running numbers for those thugs downtown, and only God knows what else they have him doing for them. She called me several times asking me to tell you to talk to Danny because the cops were going to the house all the time looking for him. They told her that they were looking for him because he was stealing bikes, breaking into houses, and stealing out of the stores over in Spanish and Dago Hill. Hell son, I even got a call from Big Bear himself. He told me he's been trying to look out for Danny until you got out, and how he always finds him hanging around the Willow Club downtown, or running the streets with a bunch of older boys. He also told me he was paying Danny to run some errands for him so that he could earn some money to eat with instead of stealing, and that the store owners and some other people he knew were complaining that Danny's out of control. They were all asking why his mother wasn't taking care of him."

After my grandmother finished talking to my father, he looked at me and asked if all that was true. As I fought back the tears, I looked at my father and wholeheartedly told him that I hated it at home, and that Mom and that guy hated me. They always told me to get out of the house to go play by Bob's, and then when I came back the door would be locked and they wouldn't open it. So, I ran downtown and looked for Big Bear and his friends to see if they needed me to do anything for them.

A bit surprised my father asked me how I got way downtown on my own anyway, since it was about five miles from the house. So, I told him that I sometimes get a ride and if not I would just walk. Then he asked what kind of things they were asking me to do. I explained that I would just deliver envelopes to a couple of different places, from Big Bear to some of the Club Guys. I told my father that every time I did something for the guys, they gave me money for food. Then with a huge smile I told my father that instead of spending all the money on food, I was saving most of it. I told him that I had a can in a secret spot so that when he came home we could buy a house of our own to live in, just the two of us, since mom's new boyfriend was living in the house now and had threatened to kill us both.

I saw the pain and anger in my Father's eyes after I told him why I was running the streets. At that moment, I knew that my father had just realized how my life was without him or anyone else to look after me. My father shamefully looked over at my grandmother and told her to call Big Bear and ask him to please look out for me until he gets out, and to tell the others that he would pay them all back for anything that I had taken. Dad also wanted her to tell him about everything that was going on at *his house*.

21

My grandmother told my father that Big Bear had already taken care of the others and that he was looking out for me, but that he didn't have four eyes. As my father nodded in acknowledgment as to what my grandmother was saying, he told her to take me home and call my mother out to the car and tell her that he wasn't happy with what was going on. Then he asked my grandmother to please take care of me if my mother asked her to. My grandmother told my father that she would if my mother asked, but he knew she wasn't in good health, and I would have to listen to her. She told my father that if she looked after me, I would have to go to school and stop running the streets.

My father sternly looked at me and said, "Son, if you go live with your grandma, you're going to have to do as you're told and if she tells me that you're not, then you're going to have to deal with me. I also want you to stop hanging out downtown so much." I looked my father in the eyes and promised I would do as he told me and obey my grandmother.

We had visited for about an hour and a half when the guards announced that visits were over. As I hugged my father goodbye I could see in his face that he was troubled by what my grandmother and I had told him. As my grandmother and I walked toward the stairs leading out, I couldn't stop thinking of how I wished that he, too, were leaving with us.

When we arrived at the house my grandmother asked me to have my mother come out to the car so that she could talk with her, so I went in and told Mom that Grandma was waiting in the car for her. My mother quickly responded by telling me to go back to the car and let grandmother know that she would be out in a minute. When I went back out to pass on my mother's message, I kissed my grandmother goodbye and after kissing me back she told me to be good.

Chapter 3

Surviving On My Own

After my visit with Dad was over, I knew what was waiting for me at home. I decided to head over to Bob's house.

Bob also came from a broken home with different men in and out of his life. For the most part, his mother was a nice lady who fed me when she could, and although I ran to her house to hide from what happened at my house, she too essentially pushed Bob and me back into the streets so that she could take care of business in her house.

As soon as I got there, I saw his mom cooking in the kitchen and nonchalantly asked her if she knew what 'aborting me with a clothes hanger' meant. Clearly, she was shocked by what I just asked her, and replied, "What?"

So, I told her about the conversation that took place during my visit to Leavenworth earlier that day. As I told her what was said, she started to cry. Since I didn't understand why she was crying I asked her what was wrong. She gently squatted in front of me so that her teary eyes were at the same level as mine and tenderly asked, "How could anyone be so cruel to a precious child like you?"

I then showed her a scar I had and asked if I was going to die. She shook her head and assured me that I was going to be fine, and told me not to worry about what was said at the visit. She told me to remember that she loved me, like she loved Bob. (*Amazingly, her kind words lifted my spirits and dismissed my concerns.*)

After that talk, Bob and I headed down the street to hang out with the other guys on the block. An hour later, we decided to go downtown to hang out at the Willow Club and see what the Club Guys were up to. We also decided to take our shoeshine boxes with us. Usually we made some easy money shining shoes for the guys that were there to see the Go-Go dancers. Although the girls were always scantily dressed, I didn't mind it in the least because I also made money shining their shoes! The dancers always paid me well and told me that I would be rich someday. The Club Guys, whose shoes I was shining that day, told me that I would end up owning their club if they didn't watch out! The girls also told them how I was a good kid and with some money in my pocket, I would be lethal. Heck, they went as far as telling the Club Guys I was more than the city could handle, and that I had already taken my father's spot! Usually they would just burst out laughing and for a few short moments, I was taken away from the heartbreak in my life and felt happiness.

I was infatuated with the Club Guys. I liked how they dressed, the nice cars that they drove, and how the dancers were always giving them money. The Club Guys always told me how having money and good looks would put nice clothes on my back. They'd tell me never to forget about them when I was rich and they were old!

It must have been close to 1:00am when I decided to get going. As luck would have it, as soon as I left the club, cops pulled up on me and told me to hold up. One of them got out of the car and said, "What did I tell you before about hanging out downtown this late? You get out of here and don't let me catch you again or I'm going to haul you in next time!"

I quickly thanked the cop, told him that I wasn't going to do it again, and started on my way home. By the time I got home, I knew the door would be locked and that no one was going to open it for me so I just slept on the porch for another night.

The very next morning, Bob and I, along with a couple of other guys on the block, headed downtown to run messages for the Club Guys. We always started out with several of the nightclubs that were on the same strip as the Willow. After that, we headed further downtown where the really beautiful women danced. They all knew me by name down there and that I was Amos' boy, but more importantly they knew that I was being looked after by Big Bear.

All of the nightclub owners were Italian and were always dressed in the best-looking clothes that I had ever seen. As soon as I walked into their Club, they'd stop whatever they were doing to ask me what I had. I would walk up to them and pass on any messages, or hand over any envelopes I had for them. Regardless of whatever I was delivering to them, they almost always had me carry something back to Big Bear. Before I left their Club, the owners made sure to tip me and told me to make sure that Big Bear knew that they had taken care of me.

Once we were back at the Willow Club, Big Bear walked me to a back room and told my friends to wait outside to keep a lookout for cops. He told them that if they saw any cops, tell the doorman and then run like hell! I remember one time when Big Bear told me that just about every cop was bad, and that they could never be trusted. He told me never to trust them or tell them anything because all they want to do is put everyone in jail.

During one of our walks to the back room, I asked Big Bear why all the guys in the club stopped to kiss and hug him, or shake his hand. He told me that it was because he was a nice guy. He said that all the guys loved and respected him because he took care of them, just like he took care of me. He told me that if I gave him my ear and kept my word, someday people would come to love and respect me when I became a man, and that I would go places in life. He also told me to keep your friends close, but always keep your enemies closer because you couldn't trust anyone.

After our talks, he let me put the envelopes that my friends and I had collected into a safe that he had in his office that was always stacked with money. I stood there gawking at all the money, and Big Bear always smiled when I looked up at him. He said, "Danny Lee, money is the root of good and evil. One day you'll learn that life is full of evil and you'll have to be a man. You'll have to use your brain to live in this world. You'll need to know how to outwit the smart and when to hide from what you cannot outwit." Then he'd put a five, if not more, in my pocket and gave me a dollar for each of my friends.

He told me to never let my friends know now, or in the future, that I had more money than they did. Since I didn't understand what he meant by that, I asked him why. He said that, "Everyone wants what you have, and what they don't know won't hurt them. This way you'll be the wise fox because you'll be safe and have a pocketful of money."

As we started walking towards the front door, Big Bear put his arm across my shoulders and asked if I knew that my Old Man was a fox. Stunned by his question, I asked how he knew my father.

Apprehensive himself, Big Bear asked, "Hasn't your father ever told you that we are the best of friends and that we go way back?"

I told him that my father must be just like me because neither of us ever told anyone that we were friends with you. I reminded Big Bear that he told me not to let anyone know that we were friends, so that way you could always have your eye on me like a Guardian Angel. By now we had reached the front door and as Big Bear slid his arm to one side of my shoulder, he turned toward me with a smile and told me that I made him proud because I was the wisest of the bunch. He told me to take care of myself and to let him know if I needed anything.

Even now as I search back to my memories of 1961, I can clearly see Big Bear driving around in his big, black, shiny Cadillac. He honked his horn while pulling over and when I heard him calling my name, I'd run as fast I could to his door. He always told me to get in and would ask me to do him a favor. He would also ask if he could do me a favor by dropping me off wherever I was headed. Either way we would chitchat the entire way. On one of our trips I remember he asked what I was doing with all of the money I was making. I told him that I spent a little on food and that I put the rest in a can that I buried in a special place where no one can get to it. He chuckled and asked why I was saving money. I enthusiastically told him so that I could buy a house for my father as soon as he came home from prison.

My words must have pierced his heart like a knife because he just looked at me and said, "You are God's child, and you're going to go places in your life when you grow up Danny Lee. Ed must be really proud to have a son like you." That's my fondest memory of Big Bear. After that day in 1961 I didn't see him, the guys, or the girls again until I was released by the state at age 15.

Chapter 4

Dumped on Grandma

That night when I got home, my grandmother was waiting for me. My mother had called and told her that if she didn't take me, she was going to call the state to come and get me. So that night, I gathered the few clothes that I had and said goodbye to my brother and sisters.

As soon as I moved in with my grandma she enrolled me in the local school. At first, like most new experiences, it seemed that I would like going to school, but as the days went by I noticed that the kids at school weren't like the kids I ran around with. Unfortunately, once they noticed the differences between us, they didn't want anything to do with me, just like I didn't want anything to do with them. For the most part, our mutual dislike didn't interfere with my attending school until somehow the other kids learned that my father was in prison. The story about my father and my family quickly spread, and that's when the teasing started. Rumors were started about how I was nothing but trouble, and most of the parents who were aware of the rumors didn't want their children associated with me. The fact that everyone made fun of my father being in prison and my mother abandoning me made me angry. I resented my schoolmates and the teachers who allowed the teasing to continue. Hostility between me and the other boys grew to the point where we traded punches several times over the relentless teasing. During one scuffle, I bit a teacher who was breaking up the fight and was immediately taken to the principal's office. He said that he had enough of me and didn't want my kind in his school. He told me that I was the devil's spawn and that he didn't know of any school that would put up with me. That day I was the only one expelled, and my grandmother was so furious that she took a thorn switch to me. After beating me, she told me to keep my hands in my pockets from now on, and if I had any problems at the next school, I was going to be in real trouble.

Trying to explain to my grandmother what was happening at school, I told her that the kids were making fun of me all the time about dad being in prison and my mother hating me. I also told her how the boys told the girls that I was a bad person, so that they wouldn't be friends with me, and that none of the kids liked me. Then I reminded her that dad told me he'd blister my butt if I ever walked away from bullies or cried if someone got the best of me in a fight. She obviously didn't want to hear it because she clenched her teeth and angrily told me that I was just like my father and that because my no-good mother let me run the streets, I was to the point that no one could control. She was so mad she went on to say that Running Wolf was the proper tribal name for me, and if I didn't do as she said, she didn't know what she was going to do with me.

The next morning, my grandmother convinced the school where she worked to take me in. Again, things were good in the beginning. I actually became friends with some of the kids who were just like the ones from my old neighborhood, but then the ones who were like the kids from the other school started making fun of me. They called me a prisoner's kid, which led to more fights. After a couple of visits to the principal's office, he called my grandmother in and told her that he was only giving me one more chance and that if I got into any more trouble, he would expel me. He told my grandmother that it wasn't just because of the fighting, but that he was getting a lot of complaints from the other parents that I was running the streets with older boys, stealing bikes, and getting their kids into trouble. I heard him ask if she had ever considered getting me some counseling so that maybe I could conform to both school and society rules. He told her that throughout all his years as the principal there, he had never seen such serious issues in a child so young. My grandmother shook her head and told him she would try to get me counseling, and thanked him for giving me one more chance.

Within a few days, my grandmother found me a counselor and after a few sessions he recommended that I see a psychiatrist. While I can't recall exactly how many psychiatrists I eventually saw, I can remember they all recommended medication to help me. Unfortunately, my grandmother couldn't afford the medications and my mother refused to help her, so I just tried my best to stay out of trouble.

For a while I was doing okay in school. One day, the teacher asked me to collect the lunch money and take it to the office. That was probably my best and worst day ever. The fact that she picked me made me so happy. For the first time ever, I was going to the office without being in any trouble. Some of the kids started to complain about me collecting the money. They told the teacher that their moms told them that I was a bad person, and that if I collected the lunch money they probably wouldn't be able to eat because I would take their money. After hearing this, I became so angry that I decided to take their money and leave just because they said I would.

As fast as I found my way back to Spanish and Dago Hill,

31

my grandmother found her way to my mother's house and told her what happened with the lunch money. She also told my mother that she couldn't take care of me anymore because of her bad health, and that she'd be glad when my father got out of prison so that he could take care of me. With a 'matter-of-fact' shrug of the shoulders and twist of her lips, my mother coldly told her that I wasn't going to last there that long because she was calling the state to come get me.

Chapter 5

Dad Comes Home

As soon as my grandmother left, I was running back to the streets with my old friends. One day out of the blue, my mother sent one of my sisters to get me so that I could go with them on a picnic. This was a huge treat for me because I was hardly ever included in any of the family outings or gatherings. I ran home with my sister and the entire family, including my mother's boyfriend, and went to the park. It was a beautiful day to be in the park, and all of us kids were having a great time playing together like we hadn't done in a very long time. We were at the park for a while when we heard what sounded like a car crash toward the top of the hill where we could see some cars passing by. Being kids, my sisters, brother and I all ran up to the hill to see what was going on.

As we were watching, I noticed a car driving up not too far from where we were standing. To my utmost surprise, it was my father! He hadn't seen us, but I excitedly called out to him, "Dad! Dad!" I knew he heard me because he pulled over. We got into his car and kissed and hugged him for the longest time. After a few minutes, he asked what we were doing in the park, so I told him that Mom and that man brought us there for a picnic. Although he coolly asked where they were, I could see in my father's eyes that he was going to get even with him for moving into his house and because my mother was going to have his baby.

At that moment, I remembered how my father told my grandmother during our last visit that he would kill the man who was living in his house and harming his children when he got out. As soon as my youngest sister pointed toward where my mother and her boyfriend were, my father kissed all of us kids. He told me to stay with him and for the others to go back and not let either my mother or her boyfriend know that they had seen him, or that he was driving around the park on his way down to where they were.

As soon as everyone was out of sight, my father jumped out of the car and grabbed a big tire iron from the trunk. When he came back into the car he told me that he was going to bust the boyfriends head open like a watermelon, and that he was only taking me with him since my mother didn't want me. On our ride to the other side of the park my father told me that he talked to his mother and that she told him how I behaved in school. Hearing the irritation in his voice as he asked me what was wrong with me. I told him that it just wasn't the same since he's been gone because no one wanted me. Mom and her new boyfriend hated me, and so did all of her side of the family. When I went to school, all the kids there hated me too. I told him how they made fun of me and always told me I was no good. I finally told him that Big Bear and the guys at the club were the only ones who wanted me around. My father put his hand on top of my head and reassured to me that he was back now and I wouldn't need to worry about those things anymore.

When we arrived at the spot where my mother and her boyfriend were sitting, my father and I got out of the car. He told me to stay there and that he'd be right back, I watched him as he walked towards the boyfriend yelling, "Who do you think you are telling my boy that he is no good and takes after me? How dare you tell a child that you're going to kill his father like a dog!"

As the boyfriend started to stand, my father went on angrily, "Plus, you take over *my* house, make love to *my* wife and now she's having your baby!" Before he could get a word out, my father swung the tire iron and hit him on the side of the head.

He collapsed to the ground and my mother, sisters, and brother all started crying. By now some other people were looking on and started shouting that they're going to call the cops. As he got up, my father hit him several more times over the head and I saw his eye pop out as he fell to the ground again. While on the ground he grabbed my father's legs, causing him to trip and fall into the nearby pond. He immediately got on top of my father and kept holding his head under the water. I feared for my father as he grabbed the tire iron out of his hand and started to hit him over the head with it. He was much larger than my father and as I watched my father bleeding and struggling for air, I pulled a big bottle out of the nearby trashcan and ran up behind him. I cocked it over my shoulder and hit him as hard as I could. Blood splattered on my face as he fell off of my father and onto the ground, unconscious. I ran to my father and helped him up.

By now we were both covered in blood and we walked up to my mother. My father slapped her across the face and told her that he was taking me with him. Angrily, she yelled, "Good! You take that brat with you and never come back around us." Since we now heard the cops getting closer, we ran to the car and drove away.

We made it to my grandmother's house without incident and my father told her that he was going to keep me with him. My grandmother asked him how I was going to be able to go to school if we were on the road and how was he planning on taking care of me if he was working. My father told her that he planned to settle down in another state and get me into a school. He also told her that he met a woman while in prison that would take care of me while he worked. Apparently satisfied with my father's responses, my grandmother told him to make sure and not wait too long to get me back into school. We were still staying with my grandmother when we learned that the boyfriend had pressed charges against my father, and that the juvenile authorities were looking for me as well, so we hit the road.

As we drove from Kansas City to St. Louis, my father told me that the woman he was now with was someone that I also knew. He told me that it was my mother's sister, and that while he was working or gone, I would have to do what she says. *Still to this day, I've never gotten over the turmoil caused by the whole situation of having my aunt become my mother.* When we arrived at her house, my father honked the horn and she came out to the car. As soon as she saw me, she asked my father what he was doing with me because she thought they were finally going to be together. My father told her about the juvenile authorities, and that the cops were also looking for him since he violated his parole. He kissed her, and as we all started to walk into the house he told her not to worry about anything.

We lived together for some time and whenever my father was away, she tried to act as though she really loved me. One day I was lying on the bed, she came over and sat next to me. She told me that I was a beautiful boy and that I should share some of my boyhood beauty with her. Since I was totally clueless about what she was saying, I asked her what she meant. She reached over and put her hand on my thigh, whispering in my ear that I should let her kiss me. She told me that she wanted to teach me some things that would help me when I was older because I was her "little man" now.

Petrified and feeling my heart pounding through my skin, I lay utterly still as my aunt raped me. At the age of 8, she raped me every day for as long as I can remember. She always finished by telling me never to say anything to my father about all the things that she was teaching me because if I did, she'd make sure that he'd let the state take me and lock me up and that I'd never see him again.

Since I once heard my father tell my aunt that she meant the world to him, I feared that if I told him, he would in fact let the state take me just to please her. Then one day I walked in on my father and aunt, and saw her doing the same things to him that she did to me. Right then and there I knew I would be in serious trouble if I ever told my father about the things that my aunt did to me while he was gone, so I kept it to myself. Even though I hated the things she did to me and made me do to her, I never told my father.

Months went by and my Aunt continued to rape me, until the day my father came home early and caught her. He beat us both and called my aunt a sick woman. He told her that she was just like my mother and desperately needed psychiatric help. He also told her that he hoped some day she would suffer for all the terrible things she did in her life, and that he was leaving. *Although I don't know why my father beat me, or what terrible other things my aunt had done in her life, that was the last time I saw her.*

That night, my father and I drove at least 60 miles to my uncle's house. It was late when we got there, and my uncle told me to lie down in the next room. I guess both of them thought I was asleep, because about a half hour later they started to talk about robbing banks. I heard them talking about getting out of Missouri and moving through the other states to pull off more robberies. They talked about hitting one side of the highway, then working their way up across the United States as far as they could before circling back down into Kansas City.

About an hour into the conversation I heard my uncle ask my

father what he planned on doing with me. My father told him that I was old enough to stay home alone until they got back, and that he was planning on taking me back to my mother since he couldn't keep running with a kid along. Even now, reminiscing on what my father said, still fills my memories of the fear I felt back then. All I could think about was how my mother told me that she would give me to the state, that the cops would lock me away, and that I would never see my father again, just as my aunt had said. I wanted to start running and never stop, but I didn't know where I was or how to get back to Kansas City. I thought if I could just get back on my own, I could ask my friend Bob if I could live with him.

The next morning my dad, uncle, and I drove for what seemed to be an eternity. Each time we stopped at a motel, they told me to stay inside and to not leave the room until they got back. Each time they returned, they'd have lots of money with them. They usually came in laughing and drinking while counting their money and would tell each other how rich they were. This continued until one day when they came back fighting over something. My father pulled a gun on my uncle and told him to take his money and leave.

Without saying a word, my uncle put all of his clothes and money into a suitcase, called a cab, and watched my father's every move as he waited. As my uncle was leaving, my father told him that he was getting away with it this time, but that next time he would kill him. My uncle responded that there wouldn't be a next time as he got into the cab and drove off.

Right after my uncle left, my father and I packed our clothes into a trunk along with whatever money was left. I asked him where we were going and he told me that we were going to visit his father in Jefferson City, the place where I was born.

Chapter 6

Dreaded Grandpa

I honestly didn't know which was the lesser of the two evils, my mother or my grandfather. I didn't like my grandfather because he was such a mean person. I remember how Grandma Amos told some of the family that he was a bastard who liked hurting others. Unfortunately, that was something I knew firsthand. Reflecting, I remember a couple of visits with him and his constant arguing with my father and mother, threatening to harm them. He usually played it off as a joke, before turning his 'jokes' on me.

He once called me into the kitchen while my mom and dad were there drinking beer with him, and put my fingers on the edge of a snap-style mousetrap. Then he said, "Tell me Danny, can a mouse get out of this trap?" before triggering the mousetrap on my fingers. The pain was horrible as I felt the spring snap the metal rod over my fingers and how I tried to get away from him. Despite the pain I didn't want to cry because my father told me never to cry and to always be a man.

As I ran from the kitchen with my fingers still pinched in the mousetrap, my grandfather ran after me calling, "You're a sorry brat and you aren't my son's child! You're a sissy, and if you lived with me, I'd make you a man like I did with your dad or I'd beat you to death!"

Even though my parents knew how mean my grandfather was, they asked him to watch over me while they went out drinking.

I begged them not to leave me there because he usually beat me, and I was terrified of him. One day, hoping to avoid another beating, I pretended to be asleep. But to my horror, instead of beating me, my grandfather got into the bed and attempted to rape me. Luckily that night my mother and father walked in just in time. My mother came into the room and saw what my grandfather was trying to do. She screamed for my father to come into the room and told him that my grandfather was trying to have sex with me. As soon as my father arrived she ran over and told my grandfather to get out of the bed and called him a dog.

Totally shocked by what was going on, my father shouted, "What the hell is going on here, Dad?"

Knowing he was caught, my grandfather tried to lie his way out of the situation by saying that nothing was going on, that he was just lying next to me so that I would go to sleep. My mother asked me what he had done to me, and I told her that he was trying to pull off my clothes and was kissing me all over my body. When my father heard that, he told my grandfather that he should kill him, and that he'd never bring any of his kids around there again. My grandfather had the nerve to tell him that we were nothing but a bunch of sick people, and that if we ever mentioned this to anyone, he'd kill us all.

With gut reaction, my father pulled his gun and pointed it at my grandfather. My mother begged my father to let it go, and that we needed to get out of there. When we got into the car, they both told me that nothing happened and that I should just forget everything that was said. They also assured me that nothing like that would ever happen again.

Remembering that incident stirs up memories of another evil experience involving my grandfather. One Christmas, my grandfather started a fight with my Uncle Joe at his house and ended up stabbing him to death. Although very old and mean as ever, my grandfather was convicted of second degree murder and incarcerated for the remainder of his life.

As fate would have it, years later I ended up at the same prison that he was in. Although the guards were aware he was my grandfather, they didn't know about the terrible things that he did to me as a boy, so they assigned me to the hospital ward where he was being housed because of his illness. Unfortunately, the fact that he was sick didn't change my feelings toward him in the least bit. Everyone on the nursing and administration staff hated to go around him because he was loathsome, so I was assigned to take care of him. Everyday, all I could think about was how I should just go into his room and kill him for how atrociously he treated me as a child. One night I even stayed up all night planning how I would report to work to take care of him as usual, and then take his life. The next day, I walked into his room with a knife in my hand and started to walk towards him. I kept thinking about how I should stab him like he had my uncle so that he could never hurt anyone else again. When I reached his bed, he looked up at me and said, "Kill me you brat. I'm better off dead anyway."

Then it hit me like a brick. "If I take his life, I'm no different than he is, and he'd be getting off easy for all the bad things he had done to people." I quickly realized that he wanted to die, so I put my knife back in my pocket and started to walk toward the door.

As I walked away he began yelling, "You're a sissy! You don't even have the guts to kill me, but if I get the chance I'll kill you, boy! You're not even my grandson, and I've known that all these years, you bastard! Your mother had so many men that she can't even remember whose kid you are!"

His words cut through me like the knife in my pocket that should have cut through him. I felt like turning back, running to his bed and stabbing him to death, but I knew that's what he wanted me to do, so I controlled my temper and walked out of his room. I went straight to the hospital guard and told him that I wanted a job change. When the guard asked about my grandfather, and when I told him that he wasn't my grandfather, he nodded his head and told me that he'd have me reassigned.

As I recall I was just 15 years old when I was transferred out of Algoa Farm, a prison in Missouri that housed young offenders, to the Missouri State Penitentiary, and shortly thereafter the state was required to release me. Not too long after that I heard that my grandfather had been released from prison because of his illness, but regrettably a short time after my release, I was re-incarcerated. The last thing I heard about my hateful grandfather was that my uncle's sons went to my grandfather's house and beat him to death for killing their father. It's still unknown who actually killed him and no one was ever charged for his death.

Chapter 7

The Set Up

On the way to my grandfather's house, my father was drinking and singing as he was driving. I was lying in the back seat of the car falling asleep when I felt the car pull over and come to a stop. I heard my father talking to what sounded to be another man outside of the car. He asked where he was going, and a few seconds later the man got into the front seat and I fell asleep again. I awakened when I felt the car pull over once more.

Although it was still dark and oddly quiet in the front seat, I saw through the space between the front seats that the man sitting in the front had his head across my father's lap. At first, I didn't understand what was happening, but then it dawned on me that the man and my father were engaged in a sexual act.

Terrified by what I was witnessing, I didn't know what to do, so I lay still as if I were asleep. Although it seemed like an eternity, it was just a few minutes later that I heard my father tell the man in the front seat to get out of the car or he'd shoot him. My father's threats intensified my terror. All I could think about were the similar threats made by my father to other people, and just wanting to get away from everyone in my family. I thought that if I could run to Bob's house, his mother would try to help me get away from all of the pain and horror in my life. My thoughts were quickly interrupted by the sound of my father's voice as he called out my name and told me to wake up and get up in the front seat. I pretended to be awakened by his call, and as I rubbed my eyes, I hopped from the back seat into the front. As I sat in the passenger's seat I saw that my father was still drinking despite being drunk already.

At this very moment, sitting in my three-man human cage with room for only one, I can't help but reflect that even though my father wronged a lot of people in his life, I can only hope that he had time to give his life to Christ and ask for forgiveness before he died. We all have good and bad in us, and my father had a good side as well.

We finally reached Kansas City and as hard as it may be to believe, my father was still drunk when he called my mother on the phone. I heard him tell mom that he wanted to come over to the house to visit the other kids and drop me off, and that she would just have to deal with me. Then I heard him ask if her boyfriend was there. I guess she must have said 'yes' because he told her to put him on the phone. My father told him that all he wanted to do was visit the other kids and drop me off, and he didn't want any problems. The boyfriend must have told him that it was okay to come over to the house and that there wouldn't be any trouble, as long as my father didn't start any. My father agreed and we drove off again.

As soon as we arrived at the house, we went right inside. There were a lot of people there and everyone was drinking. I started to get a bad feeling as I saw my father messing around with my mother, trying to get her to go into the back bedroom with him. I literally felt something wasn't right about the whole situation. Everyone was looking at each other like they were all in on a big secret.

Then I heard the boyfriend call my father out to the porch so that they could have a drink. I watched as my father got up and pulled his gun out of his pocket as he started walking toward the back porch. A minute after he went out, I heard a gunshot and I started to run toward him. As I was halfway to the porch, a lady whom I had never seen before grabbed me telling me to stay put. I bit her hand as hard and I could, breaking away to help my father. As I got closer to the door, I heard my mother yelling, "Kill that bastard!" and heard several more shots.

When I finally got to the porch I saw my father lying face down on the floor and heard him groaning in pain as the man stood over him, reloading his gun. I saw my father's gun on the floor next to him and grabbed it, but as soon as I did, the man pinned me against the banister and pushed his gun into my mouth and pulled the trigger. It felt as if my entire face was on fire. At that moment, my father started to get up and the man ran off. Once on his feet my father told me to help him to the car and to put the gun in my pocket, so that we could get rid of it later. We both stumbled out of the house to the car and took off.

Bleeding really badly and hitting cars along the way, we barely made it to Grandma Amos' house. I quickly jumped out the car, and ran to the door, crying. When she opened the door, she asked what was wrong and saw that my face was bleeding. Before I could say anything, she yelled to my uncle, who was staying with her at the time, to come down quickly because my father and I were hurt. As my uncle came down, she asked me what happened. I told her that the man had shot dad and me, and that dad was dying. As soon as my uncle heard what happened, he ran to the car and brought my father in. He laid him down on the couch. He had holes all over his body that were easily visible. My grandmother examined my face and told me that the bullet had gone right through my lip and I would be fine.

No sooner did she finish speaking when the police swarmed the house. They came in and looked at my father, and then at me.

One of them said that they needed to get us to the hospital quickly. As they put us in the ambulance, I overheard one of the cops saying that my father wasn't going to make it. On the way to the hospital my father, barely able to speak, told me to get rid of the gun and make sure that no one would be able to find it.

When we arrived at the hospital they rushed my father into surgery and the doctor stitched up my lip. By the time I was done, my mother was brought to the hospital and the cops told her to take me home. When we got home, I heard that the man had been arrested. I also heard that neither my father nor mother had pressed charges against the man for the shootings. Instead, my mother defended the man by telling police that I had gotten in the way and that the gun had accidentally gone off when I ran up and grabbed the gun in his hand. Sure enough, everyone believed her lie, and the man was released on bond. Since no one came forth to press charges for what he did, the state's case was dismissed and he beat the charges.

It wasn't until years later when I learned my mother helped him set up my father's shooting. I also heard a rumor that she told him to shoot me too if I came to my father's aid. A few years later I questioned my mother about those rumors, and she denied them completely, saying that what happened to me was not meant to happen, and that I should just forget it. Although nothing would have brought me more joy than to wholeheartedly believe my mother's words, I never talked to my mother again until a few years ago. Unfortunately, I will always believe what I've been told over the years regarding the extent of my mother's hatred toward me, which included her placing a hot iron to my head because I cried as a young child.

After the shooting, my father was hospitalized for several months, and since the incident between my father and the man constituted a violation on his parole, he was sent back to prison as soon as he was well enough to be shipped out. Soon afterward, my grandmother died.

Immediately after the burial, my mother called the juvenile authorities. Before I knew it, someone was knocking at the front door. When my mother opened the door, a man wearing a Juvenile Officer uniform came in and sat down in our kitchen. As they started to talk, I overheard my mother from the living room telling the man she couldn't take it anymore, and she couldn't take care of me. She told him that I was never home, and I was out running the streets all day and night. She also told him that I must have been stealing, because I always had money for food and new clothes, and that the backyard was full of bikes that she knew I hadn't bought. She also told him that the boys I hung out with were just as bad as I was, and that she had too many children to look after, and with another one on the way, she couldn't keep worrying about keeping me out of trouble. She told the officer that my father was back in prison, and that I was always causing trouble around the house. Adamantly, she told him to give her the papers so that she could sign me over to the state right then and there.

After listening to everything that my mother had to say, the 'Juvy Officer' told her that she needed to go to court and recount what she told him in front of the judge. Unsurprisingly, my mother didn't flinch, and quickly reassured him that she would, as long as he took me with him that night. Not a minute later, the Juvy Officer came into the living room, looked at me, and told me not to worry, everything would be alright and that I needed to go with him.

I turned from the television, looked him in the face, and said, "No, I want to go live with my father." He callously responded that my father was not around to take care of me, and said that I had no choice – that I'd have to go with him. Instinctively, I tried to run, but he grabbed and handcuffed me, then put me in his car. Although I heard my brother and sisters crying for me in the background, I couldn't block out my mother's words. Before the Juvy Officer drove off, she looked at me and with hate filled eyes, told me that she never wanted me back.

The Juvy Officer drove me to a big building where there were a lot of other kids. Once inside I was locked in a room with a mattress on the floor and a wire screen over the window. I was able to look through the screen and out of the window to see downtown Kansas City. Ten years old and scared to death, I remained in that cold, juvenile cell completely isolated from the other kids until I was scheduled to see a judge. I was fed meals in that same room which today, some four decades later, feels no different than the cage I'm currently forced to live in now. I had no way of communicating with my father, although I doubt that he would have cared about my situation, and my mother NEVER came to see me.

The only human contact that I had was the guard who fed me. He was a cruel man who often dropped my food tray on the floor and walk away. Sometimes the tray would fall face up, other times it didn't. Regardless of which way the food tray landed – that's all I had to eat. Most of the time I sat on the floor and cried, until I remembered that I shouldn't cry. Then I would divide my time looking out the window and back into the room. With the light shining through the window, it was easy for me to see that the only other thing I had in that cell besides my mattress was my toilet – an unflushable hole in the floor filled with urine and waste. All the time I was in solitary confinement I wasn't able to bathe, or given any clothes. The only thing I ever wore were the socks and underwear that I was forced to strip down to on the day I arrived.

My mother's actions ripped a hole in my heart which still today remains unhealed. Knowing that she willfully had me taken to that cold cell, and locked away made me want to lie down and die from the hurt and anger of being kept in a place like that. While the days went by, the loneliness and distress became unbearable. All I heard over and over in my mind were the voices of my grandmother, mother, and the man repeating the words, "You're just like your father." Those words echoed mercilessly in my head day after day, and when I didn't hear their voices, I'd hear the voices of the prison guard at Leavenworth saying, "If you're a bad boy, I have a room for you here in my house and you won't like living here." As everyone's words haunted me, I thought to myself – this must be like the room that I would be living in at Leavenworth. I also kept asking myself why mom told the Juvenile Officer that I was a bad kid, and that she couldn't take care of me. The constant thinking heightened my fear to the point that I truly believed that once I went before the judge, the court would hand me over to the guard at Leavenworth and that he, too, would lock me away in the room he said he had for me.

I was mortified by my surroundings. With all those thoughts running through my head, I knew that I had to try to make a run for it. As soon as they opened the door, for whatever reason, I was going to get out of there, if I wanted to stop them from putting me into anymore rooms like the one I was in. I even thought about Big Bear once telling me that if I saw any cops, to run like hell because they were the bad people, and as far as I was concerned, he was right. I was learning first-hand what Big Bear meant about the cops, and I intended to do just what he said. Knowing that, when they came to get me for court, I was going to get my chance to run like hell. I had no intentions of standing before any judge, and especially not one *who would side with my mother.*

One morning during my third week of solitary confinement I vaguely heard some of the other kids crying, while others were laughing. As I started to listen more intensely, I heard two of the guards coming up the hall. As soon as they got closer to cell I saw they were beating a kid who was with them. I couldn't believe it! He was about my size, if not smaller, and as he was crying, they threw him in the cell across from me - head first - while handcuffed. I overheard one of the guards say to the other to leave the handcuffs on until his hand turned blue, and then he might feel like taking them off. *(Although I can attest to having been the receiver of some pretty bad beatings myself, I can honestly say I have never seen anyone beaten like that before.)* As they were leaving, the one who fed me looked over to my cell and harshly said, "You see what you get here if you mess with me kid!"

After hearing his comment, the other guard asked what my story was. With absolutely no feeling in his voice, the cruel guard told him that my mother didn't want me anymore, and he'd soon have me out in front of the judge, and then my ass was his. On one hand, hearing the guard say I would soon be out in front of the judge gave me a sense of hope that I would soon be leaving that room, but on the other hand, I was even more scared because he had also said my ass would be his.

By the time the guards finally left, I was severely shaking from both fear and the cold. Thinking that I might also wind up just like the kid across from me, I called to him and said, "My name is Danny. What's yours?"

Still crying he barely uttered, "Sam." Once I knew his name I asked him why the guards had beat him, and he said it was because he kept asking to go home. Then I asked Sam why he was there. Was it because his mother said he was bad? Sam simply replied, no, he didn't have a family. He said his family took him to school one day and never came back to get him. They left him there and moved away. Right then, the lights went out. We weren't allowed to talk while the lights were out, so I quickly asked him if he was all right, to which he softly replied, "Yes." We both feel asleep crying, and that was the last time I saw Sam until some years later.

The next morning, I was taken to court and as I walked down the big corridor towards the courtroom I could feel my heart pounding uncontrollably. Then I noticed the front door leading out of the building and I heard Big Bear's voice saying, "Run like hell!" For some reason, my legs didn't want to move, but as the guard opened the courtroom door, they moved right into gear and I ran like hell out the front door.

Luckily, the guard was so fat that he couldn't catch me. It felt as if I were running so hard and for so long that I wasn't going to be able to ever stop. As I found my way back to my old neighborhood I ran straight to Bob's house. I told Bob's mother about what my mother had done, the room I was locked in, and the beating that Sam was given at the hands of the guards. She told me that I could stay the night, but that was all because she could get into trouble and the cops would then lock her up as well.

I stayed with Bob and his mom that night and made sure I was gone before they woke up. With no place to go I walked the streets aimlessly for hours. Every time I heard a car driving up I hid by running into an alley, or hiding behind trash cans or parked cars – whichever was available at the moment.

Hungry, tired, and homeless, I decided to seek refuge with some of my other friends. Over several days, I visited each of my friends one-by-one, but was always turned away. Every time I knocked on someone's door, they told me the same thing: that if they helped hide me, they would be arrested and sent to jail. Although a couple of them wrapped me something to eat before closing the door, most of them just sent me away. I had no choice but to sleep in the alleyways and pocket what I could to eat from nearby convenience stores. After almost a week with no place to stay or food to eat, I was desperate and for some reason, I thought that I could convince my mother to let me stay home for just a little while. Foolishly, I went home and to my surprise mom agreed to let me stay without much persuasion – of course as soon as I fell asleep, she called the Juvy Officers.

I was abruptly awakened by the cops and the juvenile officer who handcuffed me, and I was immediately taken back to the Juvenile Detention Center. As fate would have it, I was thrown back into the very same cell that I had fled from just a week earlier.

I was told upon my arrival that I would be going to court the very next day and that my mother would have to be there. This time they took all of my clothes, including my underwear and socks, and I was freezing. I lay on the floor shivering until I saw the sunrise and finally heard the guard coming. Along with my meal, he gave me some clothes to put on and told me that I was going before the judge. He also told me that this time I wouldn't get away and he had something special for a kid like me. Soon enough I learned exactly what he was talking about.

Fifteen minutes after he left, several guards and a doctor came into my cell and placed me in a straight jacket. The doctor gave me a shot that made me feel numb all over and really tired. They put me in a wheel chair and took me to the courtroom. Once in the courtroom, they positioned me so that I could only see one person - my mother. When the judge came in, he asked my mother to say what she had to say to the court about her son.

My mother apathetically told the judge that she could no longer take care of me because I was a troublemaker and a thief. She told the judge that I ran the streets day and night and that no school would keep me as a student because of my behavior. She closed by telling the judge that she had too many children to look after, not including the one that was on the way, and that I wouldn't obey her.

After hearing my mother out, the judge asked her if she had any idea or knew why I was that way. She replied, "Yes your honor, it's because of his father and his father's family. The majority of them have been incarcerated, or are currently in prison and they think that's a natural part of life. Also, Danny has seriously hurt the father of my unborn child just because his father told him to do so."

The judge asked her exactly what it was that I did to hurt the man she was referring to, and she told him that for no reason at all I took a bottle and hit the man in the head, splitting his head wide open. She then told the judge she was fearful that I'd hurt her next, or one of the other children. She flat out told him she just didn't want to deal with me anymore.

I felt as if I were losing my mind. I couldn't remember being as bad as I was made out to be by my mother. I sat in that wheel chair barely able to keep my head up and heard my mother saying all those things to the court, and then the judge's sentence.

"Alright the court has heard enough, Mrs. Amos, and we have a place for your son. I'm declaring him incorrigible and am remanding him to the custody of the Department of Corrections as a juvenile. He'll remain in their custody for an undetermined sentence, or until he reaches the age of 17. However, upon his release, Mrs. Amos, he will be returned to you. Since he is now ten years old going on eleven, I hope that by the time he is released, he will have changed his ways."

On that ill-fated day in 1961, the judge stated for the record that I was to be taken directly to the McCune Boys Home until I reached the maximum age limit for that facility. I would then be transferred to Boonville Training School for Boys and once I outgrew Boonville, I was to be taken to Algoa Farms where I would stay until I reached the age of 17. The judge also stated for the record that under this juvenile sentence he was imposing, if I had not shown any positive change while at the reformatory by my 17th birthday, I would be taken to the Missouri State Penitentiary where I would remain until I was released into my mother's custody.

Ask yourselves for a moment; what state of mind do you think a 10-year-old child would be in if he or she was forced into the court system at such an early age? Do you think any child should be placed in an institutional system like you view on TV, or see in a movie?

I'm sure I know your answer, but let me remind you that child #6150 spent 4 decades in the hands of the so called 'justice system.' Now at the end of my four decades, I thought I would be able to ask those here at the Federal Correctional Institution of Talladega where all the money has gone that people in society gave to assist in the rehabilitation of offenders. The only answer I ever received was, "Things have changed. We don't have money for that anymore. There is nothing we can do to help you other than give you a bus ticket to take you where you're going, and a few dollars to eat while you're on the bus." When I asked the Warden the same question, he told me, "I'm sure you'll figure it out on your own inmate!"

Ask yourself why so many offenders return to prison, and why most do so after committing crimes more serious than before.

Why has the system done absolutely nothing to help in their restoration back into society? This person then finds himself or herself faced with a panic decision. They must choose between finding a way to make a living, or returning themselves back to the hands of their tormentors in prison where at least they know how to survive. What choice do you think most would make, and who suffers?

The penal system makes it very clear that they are professionals at the jobs they have been hired to perform. They prey on the oblivious taxpayers who believe their tax money is being put to good use in order to aid in the rehabilitation process.

I hope someday to be able to address the truth of this, and I hope everyone who reads my book will find it in their hearts to do something about this terrible crime that the penal system is committing.

Chapter 8

Ward of the State

It is now 4 decades later and as I sit in this cage, I can still recall the ice-cold feeling that went through my body on that morning in 1961. By the time I was wheeled out of the courtroom, my mother had already left.

I was taken directly to McCune, and housed in a building with one hundred other boys that were my age and older. Upon arrival, I was told by the receiving guard that I could only smoke during breaks and that the daily limit, regardless of age, was nine cigarettes. He also told me that I had to follow all of the rules, take any job that was assigned to me, and that the day started at sunrise and ended at sunset.

As I passed through the processing unit, I was told by some of the other guards what would be expected of me during my time there. One guard told me that I was expected to buff the waxed floors in my unit for several hours a day by using blankets under my feet. He made it clear that I was to eat everything on my tray at each meal, and that I was to go to the gym every night to run laps and do push – ups. Another guard warned me that if I refused to obey any of the rules or do as I was told, I would be punished in any manner they saw fit. He told me that I was to walk in a double line next to my bunk, and if I failed to do so, I'd be placed in solitary confinement until he said I was ready to be released. He also explained to me that if I got into any fights, I'd be put into solitary confinement immediately. He said that solitary consisted of living in a soundproof, pitch-black cell with no heat in the winter and no window in the summer. I would only be fed bread and water for the first three days, but on the fourth day I would receive a regular meal, before the cycle would start all over again with bread and water. He continued by saying that if I ever tried to escape, or retaliated against him or any of the other guards in the institution, I'd be charged with assault and punished to no end. He told me I'd spend a minimum of 30 days in solitary confinement and then be transferred directly to the Boonville Training School for boys when they decided it was time to lift my punishment. He made it perfectly clear that they were in charge, and that there was nothing that anybody could do to help me.

The guard also told me that if I behaved, I'd be allowed to play baseball one day a week. The last guard I saw during the processing stage told me that I was expected to shower every day, change my clothes every fourth day, and switch my bed sheets once a week. He told me that my week would consist of 4 days of picking potatoes in the field, and 1 day of attending school. He said there was no TV, cards, or games to play, and that I should learn everything I could so that I could find work when I was released. He then asked me if I had any questions for him. As I shook my head, all I could think about was getting out of there. From what I had seen so far, I sure didn't like that place, and all the other boys living there seemed very mean.

On my first day in general population, two boys walked up to me and offered me a cigarette. Even though I didn't smoke at the time, I took it anyways just to fit in. I still remember that day as if it were yesterday. I inhaled my first cigarette and choked on the smoke. I couldn't stop coughing and as a result, I got sick. A couple of days later we were all put to work in the fields. The work changed everyday. One day we would pull potatoes from the ground, while the next day we were learning how to gut chickens. We would even sweep the state roads with large brooms. The guards watching us work, (who were meaner then the juvy ones) fed each of us a ham sandwich along with beans and half a cup of water.

Life at McCune wasn't trouble-free. Some of the kids had been there so long that they bullied the younger boys and newcomers. A couple of them were actually there for committing murder. Regardless of why those boys were there, they all seemed the same to me, and I didn't fit in with any of them. I tried to stay away from all of them, especially the ones who were always fighting.

For the longest time I kept to myself, until one day when one of the older boys (*he was 14 years old, a foot taller, and must have weighed twice as much as me*), walked right up to me and punched me in the face. Naturally, I had to defend myself from being hurt any further and fought back. When the guards ran into the dorm room, they grabbed us both and started beating us. They slammed our heads into the wall and told us that we would be sent to solitary for a week. Once that was over, the bully who started the fight flipped the whole incident on me by telling the guard that I was the one who walked up to him and punched him in the face for no reason at all.

Before I could set the story straight, the guard who was holding me looked at me and said," I know all about you Amos. You like to fight and cause problems, don't you? It's all in your file, boy, and we have a way to break you." He told the guard holding the older boy to let him go and sent him to his bunk. I was the only one taken to solitary that day.

The solitary cell was just as one of the guards had described it. It was completely dark, very hot, and I couldn't hear anything. Stripped of all my clothes and given a bucket to use as a toilet, I was forced to sleep on the bare floor. I felt like everyone was out to get me, and I couldn't understand why people didn't like me. I never tried to hurt anyone, yet still my mother gave me away to the state.

My first meal in solitary consisted of a small tin can of water and a piece of stale bread. Unlike what I was told in processing, I was fed the same meal for the entire time I was there. After a few days I became so hungry that I spent the rest of my time in solitary bent over with sever stomach cramps. After seven days, the door opened and the guard gave me some clothes to put on. He told me to get dressed and to bring the bucket I had so that I could clean it out.

As we walked back to the cottage, all I could think about was that older boy and how he was the one who started the fight and lied about it. I kept thinking how it was all *his* fault, but I was the only one who was sent to solitary. Since the guards would never believe me, I didn't tell them that he was the one who hit me first. I just kept it to myself and decided that if he ever hit me again, I would pummel his ass. Most importantly, I was going to make sure and do it before the guards came.

When I walked into the dorm all the other kids watched silently as the guard told me to take my bucket, (which was filled to the rim with human waste), clean it out, and go stand by my bunk. Within a few minutes he came over to my bunk and told me that the bucket was mine from now on, so I might as well keep it under my bunk for the next time I went to solitary. He finished by telling me that he was going to keep his eyes on me and if I gave him any more trouble, I'd wish I'd never met him. Then he asked me if I understood. Since I just looked at him silently, he slapped me on the head and yelled, "Can you talk now, boy?"

Not wanting to get hit again I quickly replied, "Yes." Before turning around to leave he mumbled that he could see that I was going to be a problem. As soon as I heard that I remembered my mother and everyone else telling me that I was a problem, so I just put my head down and didn't say a word. As the guard headed toward the door he looked back at me and told me to get in my bunk, and to stay there until lunchtime.

As I sat on my bunk, the bully who had punched me in the face started walking towards me saying he was going to kick my ass. I jumped right up and told him to take his best shot. Stunned by my reaction he looked at me and walked away, laughing. As soon as he was gone, the boy bunking next to me informed me he had heard the bully telling the other boys he was going to beat me up when I got back from solitary. He also told me that particular boy was always fighting with the others and taking their stuff, but since he had a family member working at McCune, none of the guards did anything to him. He even told me the bully had once stolen a guard's razor out of the staff bathroom to cut one of the other boys while he was sleeping.

After hearing of the prior events, I was really scared, especially since he had already told everyone he was going to hurt me because I fought back. I knew I had to get out of there since now I couldn't even sleep without having to worry about looking out for that bully. Later in the afternoon I learned that the bully's name was Craven, and he had been sent to McCune for killing his entire family by setting his house on fire while they were asleep. The other boys in the cottage said he was crazy; something I had no problem believing because of what he did to me.

The same day the cottage guard informed me, along with

some of the other kids, that we had to pick up the trash from the outside grounds after dinner. I wasn't usually allowed outside and really couldn't find a way out of the cottage because the doors were always locked, and the other kids were always watching what everyone else was doing. I realized that if I tried to find a way out the other kids would rat me out to the guards. So to me, having to go pick up the garbage was good news. My first thought was that I might have a chance to get away. I knew I would have to wait for the right moment and if I ran fast as hell into the woods, the guards wouldn't be able to see me in the dark. During dinner I could feel myself getting anxious. When the guard finally called out my name to join the group for trash detail, my heart started to pound like it did on the morning I was escorted to the courtroom and fled.

As soon as we were all in a group, we were taken to the outer grounds. We were given a stick with a nail sticking out of one of the ends, then told to use the nail to poke all the visible garbage lying around the grounds and drop it into the garbage bag. While I was picking up garbage I kept looking for the right opportunity to take off. As I looked around, I noticed there was a patch of woods just beyond the baseball field. I knew I would have to get closer if I was going to make a run for it. As I worked my way closer to the baseball field, I looked around to see where the guard was and what he was doing. I saw he was busy telling one of the other boys he couldn't do anything right, and was calling him names. I then looked around to see if any of the other boys were watching me, before glancing over my shoulder back to the guard. As soon as I saw the guard hit the boy he was yelling at, I knew it was time to run. I took off as fast as I could towards the woods. Behind me I could hear the kids yelling to the guard that the new kid was running away!

As I kept running I could hear the guard yelling, "Come back here! Come back here!" I ran so fast it felt like I was flying. As I made my way into the woods I heard someone jogging near by, and cars moving really fast on the highway, so I ran deeper into the woods until I couldn't hear anything around me.

Exhausted, I stopped to rest behind some bushes. I could hear the guards talking, so I knew they were fairly close. I clearly heard one of them saying, "That boy's in here somewhere, and when I get my hands on him he'll wish he had never took off on my detail." The other guards burst out laughing and then luckily for me, they all walked away. Paralyzed with fear, I dropped to the ground and laid still. As I was lying there, I recalled one of the guards telling me when I got to McCune that if anyone ran away, the farmers were paid to hunt us down in addition to the cops being called.

Once it became dark, I felt great. I finally felt free and safe from my nightmares. I rested a little longer and started to think about where I was going, and what my plan was. I knew for certain that no one would want me around because they would get into trouble if they helped me. Much to my surprise, a feeling of isolation and abandonment came over me. It hit me like a ton of bricks that I just ran away with absolutely nowhere or nobody to run to. There was no place I felt safer than here in the woods. It was just like when I lived back home - no one liked going into the woods as much as me. At that moment, I thought if I could make it to Big Bear, he would be able to help me. I knew I-70 ran between Kansas City and St. Louis and I just had to make sure I went in the right direction to get back home.

I remembered the guard who took me to McCune told another guard it was a 28-mile stretch to Kansas City, so I knew I could make it. I quietly got up and walked toward the highway. Once I was able to see cars I knew I was close enough to follow the roadside without having to leave the woods. So without a compass and no directional signs, I decided to walk towards my right.

I spent several days in the woods and whenever I got hungry, I crept up to a farmhouse. If the door was unlocked and I didn't see anyone near the icebox, I would run in, get something to eat, and run back into the woods. If the door was locked, I went to the next house. Though it was really hot during the day and water was scarce, I knew I had to keep going so I wouldn't get caught. Finally, I noticed a sign that I could see from the edge of the woods that read "KANSAS CITY" in real big letters. It felt so good to see that sign! All I had to do now was make it downtown to Big Bear's place.

I was in the woods for days without bathing, I wondered if Big Bear would even recognize me because I was so dirty. Once I reached downtown, I walked towards Big Bear's club, The Willow. The nightclub was closed when I arrived, so I ran around back and hid by the trash can. It seemed like I waited forever until I saw his big black car pull into the alleyway. I urgently ran to his door, and before I could get anything other than 'Big' out of my mouth he said, "Get in! Get in! The cops and your mother have been here looking for you! How did they know you even knew me?"

I told him I didn't know. *Maybe one of the other boys told the cops about him?* As soon as I was in the car, we drove away and informed Big Bear my mother had given me away to the State. I also told him the judge had sentenced me to the Juvenile facilities until I turned 17. I described the beatings and how I was put into solitary at McCune's. I explained that as soon as I had the chance to run, I had to take it. Amazed by what I had just told him, Big Bear asked me how was I able to find my way back. I told him I knew the highway ran between Kansas City and St. Louis, so I guessed which direction led to Kansas City. Once in town, I knew how to find my way there.

After listening to my story, Big Bear told me the cops assumed I would head back to Kansas City because they found my mom's boyfriend burned to death in his own house. The cops told Big Bear they figured he must have been so drunk that he passed out in his chair, and someone came along and doused him in gasoline and lit him on fire. They also told him they thought "I" was the one who did it.

Totally shocked by what Big Bear had just told me, I didn't hesitate to tell him I didn't kill him. I told him there was no way I could have done it because I had just got here! Big Bear told me that I must be in a lot of trouble because the cops were looking very hard for me. The cops explained to him that I was a little monster and they had to find me before I did something else. He also told me my own mother even thought I might set her house on fire. Not surprised to hear what my mother thought, I swore to Big Bear I wouldn't do that. Big Bear replied, "I know you wouldn't Danny Lee, and I know you weren't the one who killed him." But right after saying that, he looked at me real hard with a puzzled look in his eyes and slowly asked, "Did you?"

Disappointed by his skepticism I told him no, and he just smiled at me. After hearing all he had to say, I nervously asked him what he thought the cops were going to do to me. He bluntly told me if I wasn't the one who killed him, nothing. If I did do it, since I was a minor, they couldn't do anything to me. He told me he wished he could help me out in some way, but he just couldn't take care of me because he could go to jail and he was too old for that. He shook his head and said, "Here, you look like you've been through hell. Take this money and get yourself something to eat". Then he asked if I had somewhere to go, or if he could drop me off somewhere. With my eyes down, I sadly shook my head no and he said, "Look kid, you're making this old man feel real bad, but you're gonna have to get out of my car because if the cops see you with me, they'll throw me in jail."

As I opened the door I turned to look at him and saw the tears running down his face. Looking at me he said, "Your damn dad should be here in my place." With tears running down my face as well, I informed him he was back in prison. As I got out of the car he told me he knew my dad was locked up again, and he had heard about both of us being shot by that man. He said he was furious when he found out he had shot me in the mouth. He said, "You're a tough kid. You take care of yourself and just so you know, I'm glad that guy received his dues." As I closed the door, I felt like my heart wanted to stop beating. It felt as if another big hole had just opened up and I was going to die.

With nowhere to go, I started walking toward my old neighborhood. Once there, I went to Bob's house, although I knew he was probably in school. When I knocked on the door his mother opened. As soon as she saw me, she informed me that I was not allowed to come inside. She told me the cops had already been there and told her what I had done to that man.

Knowing what she was talking about, I defensively told her I didn't do it. She said, "Well, then you need to go to your mother's house and let her and the cops know you didn't do it." Then with a strange look she said, "As a matter of fact, come in and wait right here." As she walked into the next room I sat on her couch and my entire body was shaking from fear. A few minutes later, I heard cars pulling up to Bob's house, along with the sounds of many slamming doors. I jumped up to look through the front door and I could see that the cops had arrived. *The whole scene reminded me of the day my father and I were shot and the cops poured into my grandmother's house.*

As soon as the cops came inside, they grabbed me and pulled Bob's mother to the side. I could overhear them asking her when I had gotten there and if the clothes I was wearing were the same one's I arrived in. She told them I had just gotten there about 15 minutes before they arrived, and I hadn't changed my clothes at her house. While some of the cops were still talking with Bob's mom, two of them cuffed me and placed me in a police car. They went back into the house for a minute and then got in the car. Neither of them said anything to me. They drove me downtown to the police station and put me in a cell. I saw some of the cops at the station looking at me and all I kept thinking was, "Oh my God! They're going to beat me."" Just then a cop came out from one of the offices and walked towards me and said, "Hello Danny. Is it alright if I call you Danny?"

When I responded, "Yes", he asked if I wanted a soda. I quickly replied, "Yes please, my mouth is so dry." About a minute later he came back with a soda can. He opened the cell door, handed me the soda, and informed me about other people who wanted to talk with me if that was alright. As I nodded my head, he put his hand on my shoulder and said, "Okay, we're going to go in my office."

As we entered his office there were guys in nice suits all around me, which seemed comforting. One of them told me he was a detective and he needed to ask me some questions. As I sipped on my soda I told him to go ahead and ask me what he wanted. He started with, "Danny, tell us why you threw gasoline on that man and set him on fire."

When I replied to the detective, "I didn't do it," he said, "Son, some of your friends have told us it was you because you wanted to kill him for shooting you and your father." I told him I sure felt like that, but I didn't kill him. He then told me to take my clothes off so they could give me some clean ones. As I started to undress he asked, "Well, if you didn't do it Danny, then who did? Did one of your friends do it for you?"

When I said "no", he put his hand on the top of my head and said, "I believe you son." Feeling a little at ease I told him what had happened to me at McCune and how I was scared of that place. I asked him if I would have to go back there. He told me I'd have to go back before the judge and it would be up to him to decide. He asked if I remembered the judge and I said, "Yes, and he will send me back."

The detective then said, "You tell the judge what you have told us and he might send you some place else." I asked him if I could go home to my mother's house, but he told me that he didn't think so because right now they had to make sure I didn't kill that guy. He also told me there were some other nice people who wanted to talk to me about the boyfriend, so for now he'd have to take me back to the detention building where I'd stay until I saw the judge again. I told the detective I didn't want to go back to that cell and he said, "I'm sorry Danny, but we have to keep you there until the judge tells us what he wants to do with you."

As we were walking back I asked him if I was going to be punished because of what happened to that guy and he replied, "No son, I don't think you did it. Only bad people get punished." As he opened the cell door and I walked in, I turned towards him and said, "But I get punished all the time! Am I a bad boy?"

As he closed and locked the cell door he told me I was a good kid, but just had a hard way to go. He told me not to worry and everything would be fine.

Ironically after all these years of incarceration, I think back to the day when the cops investigated that murder and how they believed I was a good kid and told me only bad people were punished. Here it is 50 years later and I still can't figure out how I could be institutionalized from such an early age simply because my mother didn't want to take responsibility for me. For over 40 years I have been confined for juvenile related incidents along with my will to survive within a place that stacked the odds against me.

When the cops figured out I hadn't even ran away from McCune when that man was murdered, they officially dismissed me as a suspect. I was once again taken to the Juvenile Detention Center and placed in a cold, dark solitary cell for two weeks while I waited another court date. This time I didn't even think about running away because I realized I had absolutely no place to run to - I was so miserable and wished I could just die. Finally, I went in front of the judge and was sentenced to the Boonville Training School for Boys. The judge stated in the courtroom that he was convinced I was one of the worst cases he had ever had to preside over, and I should be put away for as long as the law allowed. After court was adjourned, I was taken to Boonville without delay.

Chapter 9

Juvy Life

Boonville was a big institution, housing several hundred boys and just as many guards. During the ride there, one of the guards told me I would never be the same again after going here, and a state prison is a better place to be than Boonville. *I guess I didn't look scared enough to him.* As fast as fear set-in, the thoughts of escape did too, and as we entered Boonville I noticed there wasn't a perimeter fence surrounding the facility. That alone increased my hope of being able to run away since by what I had just been told, I knew that I wouldn't be able to endure a place like Boonville for very long. I would rather take my chances on my own in the woods for the rest of my life than to stay at Boonville. Once in the compound, I was taken to the Administrative Building for processing. The guard escorting me told the processing guard that I was their property now, and the court hoped they could do something with me because no one else was able to.

Shortly after being processed I was taken to the Warden's office. He was a big, mean looking man. *I don't think I have ever seen a man so big in my life.* He told the guard to leave us alone and introduced himself by telling me that he was the Warden and that I belonged to him until I reached the mandatory age to be transferred to Algoa.

He then began to lay down the law. He said, "Young man, you will do what I tell you to do, and that goes for all the staff in this institution for as long as you are here. I will not put up with any trouble from you and by what I can see in your file, your family doesn't want you and no other facility can deal with you. From today on you will be known as '6150' - learn it and answer to it. In my eyes, as well as the system, you are no longer a child. Clearly, if you are big enough to get into trouble, you are big enough to deal with the consequences. You will not have any problems here unless you cause them. You will be assigned to a cottage where you will live with others your age and older.

Each cottage has 'cottage parents' who live in the building and are in charge. Since you'll be here for years to come, you'd better get use to the way things are done. This is not a summer camp and you won't be babied. You will be punished here for every wrong you do. You have been sent to me to be broken and I have broken a lot of boys just like you. Punishments at Boonville are harsher than any other juvenile facility and if you try to run from here, you'll pay dearly. I have cars and horses that will track you down and if we can't find you, the State Troopers will and THEY WILL return you to me.

Once they leave, I'll have you tied to the flag pole in front of all the other boys, stripped of your clothing, and whipped with a *cat of nine tails* as many times as I say. You will then be put in solitary for 90 days. This is my house, 6150, and you're not coming here and messing it up. On the other hand, if all goes well you will be allowed to work in the fields, or any other work detail I or my guards assign to you."

As the Warden's words played over and over in my head, I thought for sure that I would die there. I couldn't help but ask myself why mom would allow these kinds of people have me. Knowing what awaited me there, I resented my mother, father, Big Bear, Bob's mother, the judge and everyone else who hurt or tried to hurt me.

As soon as the Warden finished his pep talk, he called for one of the guards to come into his office. When the guard arrived he looked at him and said, "This is 6150, keep a close eye on him- he has rabbit in his blood and he likes to fight *(at the time I didn't know what he meant by 'he has rabbit in his blood', but now I know that it meant I liked to run away).* If you only knew the half of his file- the court sure sent me a humdinger this time. But that's okay. We'll break him like we've done with all the rest. Take him to cottage number 4 and introduce him to the Pruett's. Give them his file - they'll be tickled pink to have this one here."

The guard walked me over to cottage number 4 where we were met by Mr. and Mrs. Pruett. As we entered the cottage, the guard handed the file to Mr. Pruett and said, "This one is 6150 and he's assigned to you." Mr. Pruett flipped through the file quickly and told the guard that he would let him know if there's any trouble. As soon as the guard left, the Pruett's locked the door behind him and turned toward me. Mrs. Pruett scornfully said, "So you're the special one! Well let me tell you how it is in our house. You'll be one of 50 other numbers that live here. Since we're the bosses, you'll always address us as Mr. or Mrs. Boss. You will not talk unless you are asked to speak, and you will be punished for anything that we consider a punishable act."

I truly believe the Pruetts missed their calling in this life. They enjoyed inflicting pain and suffering so much that the Viet Cong and Nazi's were probably no match for them. While in their custody, I was forced to chew lye soap until I could blow a bubble. The soap left my gums raw and bleeding for days. I was beaten on the head with a triangle shaped oak block of wood that had the staff's name carved into it. Those beatings always caused large knots

71

and cuts on my head, yet I had to thank the Boss for making me a better person after each and every blow. One of Mr. Pruett's preferred methods of punishment was taking my head between his hands, squeezing it as hard as he could and then banging it into the sharp edge of a wooden locker, leaving open gashes.

But the Pruett's weren't the only tyrants - oh no, Boonville had an abundance of staff willing to dish out beatings. A couple of the guards used their pocketknives. They would bang the end of it into the top of my head, causing knots and cuts. Others bent me over, pulled my shirt over my head and locked it between their legs. Then they lifted their arms as high as they could and came down on my back, open handed, numerous times, which would leave their hand prints on my back for days.

After the beatings always came solitary confinement. Locked naked in a cell with no lights and a hole in the concrete floor for bodily waste, I was given an army blanket that I could use as a bed, or to cover myself. During the winter the rats came up through the waste hole and used my body to keep warm. Terrified by both the rats and the ordeal, I used my teeth as scissors and bit the edge of the blanket until I could tear strips from it. Then I bit holes down both sides of the blanket in order to weave the strips through and make a gunnysack so that I could crawl inside and prevent the rats from touching my skin. Because I tried to run away from abusive prison guards, I was often kept in solitary confinement. It seems that if I wasn't trying to fight the guards back, I was fighting for my life against the hardcore boys. A stint in solitary confinement usually consisted of 90 consecutive days on modest food portions and another 90 days with slightly more food. I was fed just enough food during the second half of confinement to give me enough strength to slave in the fields so that the state could still make their money.

For entertainment at Boonville, the guards often forced the boys to fight each other until one of them went down, just like the gladiators of Rome. And when not working from sun up to sun down or in solitary confinement, we were usually forced to stand in one spot bent over holding our ankles for hours on end. If we moved or fell over from exhaustion we were beaten right back into position and the clock started all over. My time at Boonville was very hard to endure, and most people can't even begin to comprehend the extent of torture and abuse inflicted by guards and other staff members. Juvenile offenders are legally held captive and systematically tortured at facilities all over the country. Often fearing for their lives, they have to watch out for other boys and guards alike.

As I became older I was asked by the Warden to participate in a program intended to help parents of high-risk children to keep them out of the juvenile system. I was instructed to convey to these parents the facility's view of 'what it was like in Juvy.' In other words, they didn't want me to tell the parents about all the torture and abuse that really went on behind those doors. But of course I told them the way it really was, and ALL of the parents that I ever spoke with said, "My child will never have to go through this." I tried to make it as clear as possible to those parents that the system is not prejudiced, and that everyone is mistreated in the same way. I told them very clearly if their children entered a juvenile facility, they would be tortured and abused, and there was nothing that they could do about it. Needless to say, once the Warden got wind of what I was really telling these parents, I was put in solitary and the program was discontinued.

After spending several years confined at Boonville, I became more and more indifferent towards the abuse and torture. While there, my moral judgment toward the other boys and guards was so indifferent that I was considered a threat to the orderly running of the institution and was moved into other cottages. I was housed in a cottage with much older boys who were considered extremely violent and the threat of harm was even greater. I got into so many fights with boys who thought they could take advantage of me in one way or another. I became hardened. Often the fights became entertainment for the guards who regularly instigated the attacks upon me. I suffered countless stab wounds and severe beatings at the hands of hard-core juvenile offenders while at Boonville.

Once healed, I would return for revenge. Sometimes I was successful, and other times I found myself being awakened in the infirmary. Of course, each hospital stay was always followed by another stint in solitary. But I didn't let this bother me, and continued to take my position and target those who had harmed me. Educated by both the guards and thugs, I attacked without warning like a wild wolf whenever I saw the opportunity to make my move.

For many years, the guards would quietly open my cell door open in the middle of the night, and jump me while I was sleeping. They struck in numbers to make sure that I remembered the beatings, and they left me curled up on the floor in pain. They always told me that they'd be back to give me more when I least expected it and walked out of my cell, enjoying the fact that I was powerless against them. Actually, that happened so often that it got to the point where I had to tie a strip of sheet around the bars of my cell door before I went to sleep so that the guards couldn't sneak in. My precautions only seemed to infuriate them more. The guards would use manipulation to encourage the other boys to do their dirty work for them. *I honestly think that the guards preferred it that way, because they knew that I would take revenge against the other boys.* It really was a vicious triangle.

Eventually, the only thing that I saw in front of me was an enemy. I viewed all the other boys and guards the same. There was absolutely no difference between the two because I had suffered at the hands of both. Even though I had no where to run, I always tried running just to show them that I still could, and to prove that they hadn't broken my spirit despite all the torture and abuse. After being *molded* for years by the juvenile system, I learned that both groups (the guards and other boys) eventually viewed me as dangerous, so for the most part they left me alone. However, there were always one or two bad asses that felt like testing me, but I always fought back at them with more than they could handle. But unlike them, I could deal with solitary confinement without any qualms for my participation in the *fun.*

By the time I was 15, I had given up all hope of ever getting out alive and truly believed that I would be institutionalized for the rest of my life. I was ultimately transferred into a maximum-security cottage where I met up with the boy whom I had long forgotten. *When I was 10, he had been badly beaten by the guards in the juvenile detention center for wanting to go home and thrown into the cell across the hall from me.* Sam pulled me aside and gave me the lowdown on everybody. He told me that he had been there for five years, and I told him that's how long I had also been at Boonville.

He said, "I've built up a really bad record and don't think that I'll ever get out, KC." *(By now I'm no longer referred to as Child 6150, or Danny. The other boys quickly nicknamed me KC because whenever something involving me kicked-off they would say, "It's that guy from KC again").*

When I told Sam that I felt the same way, he responded, "Well, KC, what are you gonna do about it?"

That day was a turning point in my life. Sam had managed to

sneak in a jar full of gasoline that he had siphoned out of one of the State's cars while he was on work detail. He put the jar in my hand and told me that he'd been sniffing it all day. He told me to give it a try, and that it would help me forget everything. Although I had never used drugs or any other mind-altering substance, I decided to get high for the first time. The first few sniffs made me feel a bit of nausea, but after a couple of minutes, a strange- violent feeling came over me. Within a few minutes, Sam and I were both feeling and behaving the same way. I saw that the other boys knew there was something different in our actions, and noticed they were staying as far away from us as possible. What they couldn't see was that within those few minutes, Sam and I became a team.

From that day on we formed a bond and stood back-to-back in our prison wars against the guards and inmates alike. Soon afterward, we began hearing rumors that we would soon be moved to Algoa Reformatory (*an adult prison*) because of our joint rebellion against the system. As soon as we got wind of the rumors, Sam and I vowed that when the time came we would jump the night guard, take his keys, and make a run for it.

As time went on, Sam and I continued to get high and hold our own against *the system.* On one particular day, Sam and I were sniffing gas from early in the morning until late in the evening. Later that night Sam said, "Hey, KC. Remember that low-life guard that nearly beat me to death a while back? Well, he's on night duty in our cell block tonight - how about we jump him as soon as he dozes off, and then make a run for it?"

Having been on the receiving end of a few beatings by that guard, and high as a kite to boot, I had absolutely no problem buying into Sam's plan to sneak up on him and knock him out. I told Sam I was "in", and that we should plan our escape before we struck. We

76

went back to my cell and decided how we were going to blow that joint. Since my cell was the closest to the guard's station, I kept watch to see when he dozed off. As soon as he fell asleep, I snuck out of my cell and ran down three doors to Sam's cell to let him know that it was time. "Let's go, KC, it's on!"

We bolted with nothing but our pajamas on and bare feet so that we wouldn't make any noise. When we reached the guard's station, we saw his head down on the desk over his folded arms. I tiptoed over to the wall and grabbed his time clock off the hook. *(As I turned toward Sam to let him know that I had the clock, I noticed that he was holding a long shard of glass rapped in a rag. I just figured that he brought along it to scare away any of the other boys if they approached us so I didn't give it much thought.)*

I raised the time clock as high as I could, and slammed it into the back of the sleeping guard's head. As he fell to the floor, I grabbed the keys that were on his desk. I ran downstairs to the front door as quickly as I could, and started trying all the keys to find the one that would open the lock.

As I'm almost out of keys to try I said, "None of these keys work on this lock." *(As luck would have it, I later learned that the guards weren't given keys to the front door. They were only given keys to the cellblock and had to wait for the next shift change to be let out by the incoming guard.* When I didn't hear a response or acknowledgement of any sort, I turned and saw that Sam wasn't behind me as I thought he was. Knowing that I couldn't open the door, I figured that the only other way to get out was to squeeze through the windows on the door. Although the windows were covered with chicken wire, I knew that we could kick them out with our State boots that would also protect us from cutting our feet. Since Sam wasn't behind me, I assumed that he was upstairs

77

watching over the guard to make sure that he didn't wake up before we were able to open the door.

I was so high from sniffing gas all day that it was really hard for me to run back upstairs to let Sam know that none of the keys had worked, and that we were going to have to get our boots on to kick the glass out the doors. When I finally reached the top of the stairs I ran over to the guard station and saw that Sam was covered in blood. As I went in and looked down at the guard, I saw him lying face down in a pool of blood. Totally shocked by the scene, it took me a minute to realize that Sam had used the piece of glass that he was carrying to stab the guard. Judging by all the blood on Sam, and by the pool of blood on the ground surrounding the guard, I figured that the guard had to be dead. I looked at Sam and told him that we had to get our boots and leave now, but he appeared frozen in time and just stood over the guard looking down at him.

I stretched out my arm, nudged him on the shoulder a couple of times and said, "Sam! Come on! Snap out of it. We've got to go now." After a few seconds he finally looked up at me. I told him about the keys not working and that the only way out would be to kick out the glass and squeeze through the windows in the door. As he nodded I asked why he killed the guard.

Despondently he replied, "You know, that miserable guard nearly killed me two years ago KC, and laughed about it. I had to pay him back." Shaking my head, I told him to come on! We were really in a lot of trouble. I told him to wait for me by the door while I went to get our boots. As soon as I ran to my cell to grab my boots, I heard the sound of glass breaking. I ran downstairs as fast as I could. When I got to the door, I saw Sam standing in a pool of blood. Apparently he kicked the glass out with his bare foot, and it looked as though the glass went right through his leg and almost completely cut it off. I quickly squeezed out the window, and then pulled Sam through. So much blood was pouring out of his leg that he could barely stand, so I put him over my shoulder and carried him. After a fairly long way, I couldn't go any further and had to stop. I put Sam down and frankly told him, "You're going to bleed to death, and I can't run as fast while I'm carrying you. You're slowing me down, man, and the guards are going to catch us both. Man, why did you have to go and kick out the glass without your boots on? I told you that I was going to grab our boots and to just wait for me at the door. Now I'm going to have to leave you here. I don't want to Sam, but you've given me no choice." He told me not to worry about him, and that he'd rather die than to stay at Boonville any longer. I dragged him into the woods, leaned him up against a tree, and told him that no one could see him there. I told him that I was sorry, but I had to go. He nodded and said, "I know you do KC. Just go and don't let them catch you." I sadly said goodbye to my friend, turned away, and bolted.

I ran and ran for what seemed like forever. It was cold out that night and all I had on were my pajamas and State boots, but I kept on running. I finally made it to the highway and spotted a tractor-trailer that was hauling boats that was pulled over on the road. It was facing towards Kansas City on I-70, so I snuck out of the woods and onto the edge of the highway, keeping a close lookout for the State Troopers and guards. As soon as there was a break in the traffic, I ran across the highway and headed toward the back of the truck.

When there was another break in the traffic, I quickly crawled to the top of the truck and into one of the metal boats. I lay there waiting for the truck to get on its way so I could hitch a ride to Kansas City. No sooner had I settled into my boat, than I heard a car pull up next to the truck. I then heard a door open and slam shut, followed by the truck driver asking, "What's the problem officer?" I knew it had to be a trooper he was talking to. The trooper ignored the trucker's question, and asked him if he had seen a young man wearing state issued clothing that had just run away from the Boonville facility in the area. When the trucker replied, "No", the trooper told him to keep his eyes open and to give them a call if he came across anyone fitting the description   As soon as the trooper got back into his car, the trucker started his truck and we drove off.

Now, I was really getting cold because the wind was hitting the metal boat, making it freeze up. Though my skin was starting to stick to the boat, all I could think about was reaching Kansas City. I figured that as soon as we pulled in, I would climb down and start running, but unfortunately the cold had caused me to fall asleep. The next thing I remember, I was waking up in a hospital ward. As soon as I opened my eyes, I saw a state trooper and what appeared to be a hospital security guard standing at the door. They were close enough to me that I could hear them talking. I overheard the State Trooper telling the security guard that the other boy almost lost his leg, and that the C.O., (corrections officer) who had been stabbed several times with a piece of glass, barely survived the ordeal.

The security guard then asked the State Trooper if I had been the one who stabbed the C.O. The State Trooper told him no -that it wasn't me. I was being treated for frostbite. He went on to say that the boy who almost lost his leg confessed to being the one who nearly stabbed the C.O. to death. The security guard then asked if we would both be going back to Boonville. The trooper shook his head and told that we would probably be taken directly to Algoa where the one who did the stabbing would be charged with attempted murder and I would be charged with escape. He told the guard that both of us were problem cases, and that he'd be surprised if we didn't get ourselves killed in the big house.

As soon as we were able to make the trip, Sam and I were sent directly to Algoa and immediately separated. During processing, I was informed that I had been sentenced to serve two years at Algoa for escaping from Boonville. As a new arrival I was placed in solitary, but as weeks went by I was given no indication of when I would be moved out of solitary and into the general population. After about six months, I was informed by a social worker that I would be serving my entire sentence at Algoa in solitary confinement with very limited human contact. A few weeks later I had heard from an inmate who had just come into solitary, that almost immediately after arriving at Algoa, Sam was convicted of attempted murder. Although he was a juvenile, he was sentenced as an adult for stabbing the Boonville guard. He also told me that because of the nature of the crime, he was transferred directly to the Missouri State Penitentiary in Jefferson City.

A year and a half into my sentence the same inmate re-entered solitary and mentioned that he heard that Sam had been at the penitentiary for only a short time before being sent to solitary, and that it was rumored the guards took advantage of the opportunity to get revenge. He told me that while in solitary, Sam was beaten to death. I broke down and cried when I learned of his death. While everyone around me just wanted to explain my demeanor as that of a *problematic kid,* Sam was the only person in my life who knew what I endured all those years and why I became the person that I was. Because he lived the same life that I did, Sam understood that it was a matter of surviving your surroundings, or die.

After completing my two-year sentence in solitary at Algoa, I was transferred to the Missouri State Penitentiary where I remained until I was released back into my mother's custody. It took *the system* a couple of weeks to process the paperwork and finally at the age of 17, I was allowed to walk out of the Missouri State Penitentiary. I was instructed to go to the front entrance gate where the guard that was assigned to drive me to the bus station was waiting for me.

When I walked up to the guard I handed him my paperwork and he told me to follow him. We walked right over to one of the department of corrections vehicles and got in. On our way to the bus station, the guard asked what I had learned throughout all the years in different institutions. I just looked at him real long and hard and heatedly said, "I learned that I must have done something really bad once and went to hell for it."

Chapter 10

Homecoming

Nothing else was said during the ride until we reached the bus station. As the guard handed me a one-way ticket to Kansas City, he asked if I was going home to Linda. Taken back by his question I asked him how he knew my mother's first name. *What happened next is something out of a soap opera and has haunted me still to this day.* He casually said, "I'm her brother. Give her my regards, and good luck kid. My name is Uncle Wayne." I was so stunned by what he said that I couldn't even move. I guess he could see how shocked I was by what he had just told me, so he just signaled for me to close the door and drove off.

Numbly, I walked over to the Kansas City bus, gave the driver my ticket, and fell into the first empty seat I could find. All kinds of thoughts were going through my head during the ride, but the main one was that my mother's brother knew that I was imprisoned at the same facility where he worked. Not once did he ever come speak to me, or for me. Strangely enough, he was the one assigned to drive me to the bus station. I then thought, 'Why should he care enough to come speak to me when he's from my mother's side of the family? After all, none of them like me because they think that I'm just like my father - whom they all hate.'

I decided that the first thing I was going to do when I reached Kansas City was to ask my mother why she let me suffer like I had.

Then I was going to go ask Bob's mother why she called the cops on me when she could have just told me to leave and to never come back. After that I planned on finding my running buddies from when I was 10 to find out who lied to the cops about me by telling them that I burned my mom's boyfriend alive. As I kept thinking of the things I was going to do when I got back, it dawned on me that even if I got bad answers from everyone, it wouldn't change anything that had happened to me while I was away. It just wasn't worth it.

So before I reached Kansas City, I made up my mind that I wasn't going to ask anyone anything. I just wanted to go home, see my mother, brother and sisters, and go downtown to visit Big Bear and the club guys. I thought that maybe I could ask Big Bear for a loan so I could buy myself some clothes. I also wanted to ask if he had any work for me so that I could get a place of my own to stay.

When the bus finally pulled into the Kansas City station, I looked out the window hoping that maybe Mom, or someone else would be there waiting for me. But, since no one was there for me, I started walking to my mom's house. When I reached downtown I decided that since I was already in the area, I should stop and see Big Bear and everyone else first. As I kept walking towards the Club, I could see that nothing had really changed during the 7 years that I was away. I also found myself feeling a little scared and out of place and although I couldn't explain why, I felt lost.

I could see the Willow Club just ahead. The lights were on and people were going inside. Instead of walking in myself, I walked up to the window and looked through. *Funny, when I was sent away I couldn't reach the top of the window to peek in, and now I could see right through it with no trouble.* I looked behind the bar and saw Bob standing there, so I knew that Big Bear must be in the back office. I then decided to go inside. As I started to walk through the front door, a big guy wearing a fine-looking suit put his hand up in front of me and asked for an ID. When I told him I didn't have any ID and I was only there to see Big Bear, he yelled over to Bob and said, "This kid says he's here to see Big Bear, do you know him?"

As Bob was walking over I could tell he didn't recognize me. I couldn't blame him since the last time he had seen me was when I was ten years old. When he got to the front door he looked at me and asked for my name. Nervously, I told him the last time he had seen me was 7 years ago, and everyone at the club knew me as Danny Lee.

Enthusiastically he yelled out, "Oh my God!" His yell was so loud that Big Bear came out from the back room to see what was going on. As soon as he saw me, he came up to me and grabbed me. He gave me the biggest hug I've ever received and then turned to everyone and said, "My kids always find their way back to me."

He turned back towards me and said, "Come, come. We have a lot of catching up to do." As we walked into his office he said, "How are you doing, Danny Lee?" I replied, "Well Big Bear, for starters, my name is now KC."

"KC," he responded, "Why the name change?" I told him I had earned it during my 7 years of suffering. He looked at me and said, "I see son. Okay. KC it shall be." He then asked me how long I had been released for, and if I'd eaten or been home yet. Shaking my head, I explained to him I had just got off the bus and headed straight here to see him.

With a big 'Kool-Aid' smile on his face he said, "My boy! My boy has come home." I know you must have been through hell son, and I won't pry, but if you need anything at all, you just ask and you got it."

I seized the opportunity to ask for a loan so I could buy

myself some food and clothes. I also told him I needed a job. He didn't hesitate a bit to say, "Sure, let me get you some money."

As he reached into his safe and handed me a wad of cash, he told me the cops and Feds had come down on him so hard that they put him out of the envelope business, so now he just played the tracks as a hobby. He told me not to worry about paying back the money, but if he needed something, he'd send for me. He asked if I was going to be staying with my mother. I told him that even though I was released into her custody, I hadn't seen her yet and didn't know if she was going to let me stay at the house, but I would stop by the club regularly.

As Big Bear looked at me, he told me he could see in my eyes that I had changed. He expressed to me how he was sorry about everything that had happened to me, and that it should have never happened in the first place. He told me he was there for me should I ever need to talk about anything. Then he asked, "What about your old man? Is he still in prison?"

I told him I didn't know since no one came to see me while I was away, so I really didn't know much about anything. He understood, and we said our goodbyes to each other. I left the club and went to the store to buy myself some clothes, and then took a cab to my mother's house. *I can't help but think back to the old block and wonder what ever happened to the guys. Who ran the envelopes in my place when I was gone? I wonder what happened to my dog... the one the man threatened to shoot, and the money I had hidden away in a can. I even catch myself thinking about Craven - the boy who had punched me in the face for no reason at McCune. Unlike others from my past, I actually know what happened to him. He eventually ended up in Boonville, where his life ended within a year of arriving. He was shot and killed while trying to break into someone 's house after escaping from Boonville.*

When the cab pulled up to my mom's house, I got out and paid the driver. As he drove off, I looked at the house and couldn't help but notice someone was looking at me from out of the window. I started walking towards the house, and as I got closer I could see the face in the window was that of an unfamiliar girl. When I reached the door and knocked, the same girl who was looking out of the window answered the door. Standing there not recognizing the little girl, I thought maybe mom had sold the house and didn't tell anyone at the Department of Corrections what her new address was in order to never see me again. The girl looked up at me and said, "Bub?" *Back then 'bub' was short for brother.*

I replied, "Yes, Who are you?"

Grinning, she shouted, "Your sister, Abby!" Embarrassed I quickly said "I'm sorry, I didn't know it was you, sis!" Shortly after, Monica, Paul, Amanda and Cheryl, (the man's daughter), had came to the door to see me and tell me who they were. Abby yelled out, "Mom! Mom! Danny's home!" Standing there I couldn't believe how big and different my sisters and brother looked, and how Cheryl wasn't even born when I was sent away.

As Mom came into the front room, she just stared at me for a while. She then walked over to where I was standing to look at me some more. Finally she said, "Danny, you're so tall now and you have changed so much. Can I have a hug?" I looked back at her and asked if I could stay there, or if I had to leave. She didn't say anything for the longest time.

I said, "Alright," and looked down at Abby and the other kids. "I'll see you around." I turned and walked right out of the house "Where am I going to go now?" I thought.

As I'm about halfway down the block I heard Abby calling to

87

me, telling me to wait. I stopped, turned around, and waited for her. When she caught up, she told me about my friend Bob who lived on the next block over, and how he now had a place of his own. Bob lived there with his girlfriend and some other people. The rest of my siblings had followed Abby out of the house as well, and we all hugged each other for a moment.

"Bub," Cheryl said. "I've been saving this blanket for you for the longest time so you wouldn't get cold." As she handed me the blanket I looked at her and said, "Thanks sis, and I love you too." After we said our goodbyes, everyone except Abby headed back to the house. Abby told me to follow her so she could show me where Bob lived.

As I followed Abby down the street, I had flashbacks of our younger years and how we used to always follow each other around. I specifically remember how Abby used to suck her thumb, and how we even ran away from home together one time. Abby was just 5 at the time, and I was 7. In the middle of the night we dragged a chair across the floor and pushed it up against the front door so that we could reach to unlock it. We opened the door, and ran and ran until we finally crawled into the back of an unlocked car that was still running. When the owner came back outside, he saw Abby and I just sitting there. The man told us not to worry, and that everything was going to be just fine as he drove us to the police station. It didn't take the cops long to figure out who we belonged to, and they called our mother to come get us. Boy, did we get our butts whipped when we got home! I still can't help but smile to myself whenever I think back to Abby and her thumb, or to Cheryl and the blanket that she had saved for me for so many years.

When we reached Bob's house, Abby knocked on the door. A woman answered the door and said, "Hey Abby! Who's that with you?" Abby told her I was her brother Danny, and that I was a friend of Bob's.

At that moment, Bob came to the door and yelled, "No way! Is that you Danny?" I responded, "Yeah, Bob, it's me! But no one calls me Danny anymore - its KC now." Bob smiled as he said, "Huh? KC, what did they do to you in prison? Change your name?"

Smiling back at him, I told him I had earned it. Everyone looked at me with curiosity, but none of them asked what I meant by saying *I had earned it*. Bob told me to come inside, and offered me a beer. As we sat in the living room drinking, I told him about my time in prison. With every word I spoke, I could see the shock intensifying in his face. We all talked for a little while longer, until it started to get late. Knowing I had nowhere to go, I asked if I could stay with him for a few days until I could figure out a plan. He didn't hesitate to say yes.

Abby then came over to me and said, "Bub, don't worry about Mom. You're better off on your own. I've gotta go now, but I'll see ya' around."

Once Abby left, Bob and I caught up on what had happened in his life since I had been away. He told me how his mother had thrown him out of her house because he had started using dope, and that he started standing up to some of the men she brought into the house. He also told me that similarly to my home life, different men were always coming and going. He even described a few incidents where he had to bust a couple of the men up for beating on his mother. He described how his mother would then beat him for driving them away.

He said, "To be honest KC, it got to be so bad between the dope and the men, she rented this house for me so I would stay away from her house. She told me as long as I stayed out of her life, she would pay the rent and I could live here with whomever I wanted. So here I am, man, and now you can stay with us as well."

I couldn't help but look around the apartment and think to myself, 'My God, all these kids live here? This place looks worse than some of the cells I've lived in.'

Bob smiled as he told me that he wanted to introduce me to this really nice girl. He told me she was the only one there who didn't have a boyfriend. Putting his beer down, he signaled for this girl who was in the kitchen, to come over. As she started walking towards us, Bob said, "Come here. I want you to meet my old running buddy who I've known all of my life. He is a real good dude!"

"KC, this is Jasmine," Bob said.

I smiled as I looked up at her and said, "Hi." She replied with, "Hi KC," and we all started talking.

After about 15 or 20 minutes, Bob asked if I wanted to get high. "With what?" I replied? "Speed," Bob answered coolly. I had never been high on *speed* before, so I said, "I guess I'll try it." I soon noticed everyone in the house came nearer and nearer to us, as if they apparently wanted to get high as well. I figured it must be some good stuff! I asked Jasmine if she got high very often, and she nodded affirmatively. Not knowing what to do I watched as Bob and Jasmine sniffed some *speed* up their nose through a straw, and when they passed it to me I did the exact same thing. After everyone had had their turn, we started drinking again. I remember feeling really excited and alive- it was nothing like the high I used to get from sniffing gasoline with Sam. Some time later, Bob asked me if I wanted to do some *coke*. I told him that I never had it before, but was open to trying it. He explained to me that I was going to love it, and that I didn't know what I had been missing. Subsequently, I tried it and he was right- I liked it!

As we spent the night getting high and drinking, I felt wonderful. Although I hadn't slept or eaten in over 24 hours, it didn't phase me in the least. Bob then told me he had something even better than *coke* and *speed*. Before I knew it, he got up and left the room. Within a few minutes he came back with a small clear plastic bag filled with a brown substance. He scooped some out onto the table and asked, "Have you ever used *heroin*?"

Jokingly I said, "Man, the only thing I have used to get high was gasoline while I was in the joint!" Everyone burst out laughing. "Well, try this man. This is great stuff," Bob explained. I sniffed it up through my nose like I did with the *coke* and was immediately high. Even though the *heroin* made me real sick at the time, the resulting high I would get was well worth it.

Despite knowing that Bob meant well, offering me those drugs was the worst thing he could have done for me. Unfortunately, about 3 years after that day, Bob overdosed and died. Sadly, like me, the only relief to Bob's childhood pain and suffering came through the chronic use of drugs, and although I've been drug-free for years now, that fateful day was the beginning of a decades long drug addiction.

Jasmine and I quickly became friends and started dating, and before long we were 'officially' a couple. *We were a strung out couple that had a relationship built on booze and drugs.* Although I knew I had to find work to support both of our habits and to pay our rent to Bob, I soon found out that no one wanted to hire someone that had been confined as a child for such a long period of time. Every job I applied for resulted in the same response, "We'll call you," yet I never received a call.

I was able to get a couple of jobs from Big Bear until he found out that I was strung out on dope. He told me that he couldn't keep giving me work unless I cleaned up because he couldn't afford for his business partners to see me in such a state. Before long, I felt as if I was at the end of the road with nowhere to turn and decided I had to do something.

As luck would have it, I walked up on Bob and some of the other guys from the neighborhood that were already high and drinking. It wasn't long before one of them suggested that we should just start taking what we needed. Of course, it didn't take much convincing for me to buy into that idea; I already believed that this world had taken enough from me. I had every intention of listening to the little voice in my head that was saying, "Go for it KC. It's time that you get yours."

We didn't waste any time getting started. We were stealing everything and anything we could get our hands on. We became a pack of wolves who were robbing the local stores, businesses, cabs, drug dealers, homes, and even cars that we would take to the chop shops. Eventually, we started thinking about moving up into the big leagues, and we should consider robbing a bank. At this point in my life I found myself in a situation where I couldn't find any way out. It was a one-way street.

Shortly after that, Jasmine told me that she wanted to get married. Right out of the blue she comes to me and asks, "Are you ever going to marry me, KC?"

Taken off guard by her question, I answered, "Jasmine, how can we get married? I don't even have enough money to get us out of the jam we're in now!"

"But I want to get married!" she explained. Trying to reply the best way I could, I replied, "Jasmine, listen. I've been doing a lot of bad things, and if the cops ever catch up with me, I'm finished. I'll be sent to prison and you'll be married to someone who'll be locked up for a long time." That response was clearly a waste of time since she made it perfectly clear that she wasn't going to take *no* for an answer. To help drive her point home, her mother insisted that if we were going to be living together we ought to be married. Her father also joined the bandwagon by telling me he knew that I was having sex with his daughter.

At age 17, Jasmine and I got married. In trying to keep with tradition, I wanted to take her on a honeymoon. I went out to make more money and once I had enough saved, I made plans with Bob, his girl, and a couple of other friends to head to Florida. Of course we didn't have any means of getting there, so I told everyone not to worry and I would go out and get us a car. I headed straight for a car lot and stole a brand new car and later that day we all packed up and headed to Florida. We all chipped in some money and rented a place to stay down there. We were all having a wonderful time, but after about a week we decided to head back home. On our way out of Florida however, the State Troopers were hot on our tail. I unsuccessfully tried to outrun them, but failed. Busted, I owned up to stealing the car and was taken to jail. Jasmine and everyone else were put on a bus and sent back to Kansas City.

As I sit here today in my cell, I find myself thinking about how hard it was to find work after I was released from prison at 17 years of age. No one wanted to hire me back then, and now after all these years spent in prison, I am about to be released again at the age of 64, having spent over 40 years in prison. I read in the USA Today (Monday, July 23, 2007 issue, page 3A) in big bold print, "EX-CONS SENTENCES DON'T ALWAYS END IN RELEASE. It goes on to express that criminal records can limit aid opportunities once released and ex-offenders must be held accountable and accept that in addition to their incarceration that they're illegal behavior

93

may cause other ramifications.

I can only remind you again that the 'system's' actions, along with their money-making business, greatly affect these offenders. These prisoners are human beings. They are all family members; sons, daughters, husbands and fathers, etc. They are all used as a product in order to make money! This article in USA Today should show you that this is all a plan to make prisoners worse off people, and then release them upon society. It's as if they make sure that the prisoners have no choice but to resort to any means necessary in order to fight for survival. The odds are completely against them. Where is our help?

Chapter 11

Descent into Hell

After being officially charged with grand theft auto and taking the stolen vehicle across state lines, (which makes it a federal offense), the FBI became involved. They picked me up in Florida and took me back to Kansas City where I was imprisoned and awaited sentencing. Since I was only 17, the Judge I went before decided to release me on bond and reschedule my court date, as opposed to sending me back to prison.

As soon as I was free, I decided it would be better if I didn't return to court to have my case heard. I made the decision to jump bail, and ended up running from the FBI for over a year. They finally caught up with me one night when the FBI agents busted in on us while we were sleeping. As Jasmine and everyone else watched, I was handcuffed and taken away. I lost sight of her as I was led out of the house and I felt a new hole in my heart. I was sent to the Jackson County Jail (which was actually a prison within a jail) to await sentencing. Jackson County Jail was a place where the established convicts ran everything. Once again I found myself in the very same environment that had changed me from a mischievous boy – "Danny" into a warrior against the enemy – "Running Wolf".

At the County, I was sent to the 'tank'. *The tank is a long cellblock constructed of steel that resembles a submarine. As soon as you entered the tank, the guard would call out 'fresh meat' to let everyone know that someone new was coming in. Immediately, the vicious veteran convicts (the one's who have spent their lives in and out of prison and were respected for their actions, known as 'Key-Cell Convicts') came to the head of the tank to greet the new comers. They didn't hesitate to let you know who was in charge and about the people who had been killed in there. Trust me - it was crystal clear to everyone that THE GUARDS WERE NOT THE ONES IN CHARGE. Every new inmate was also forced to donate a specific amount of money to the 'Poor Box' (a box that was hung from the cell bars to mainly keep the Key-Cell Cons off your back). Smokes and coffee were also put in the box for the rest of the tank's inmates to use as a good gesture. If you didn't contribute, you'd have a really rough time while in the tank. The Key-Cell Cons would prey on those who didn't have a connection to a 'top dog' convict, and depending on your prior record and how well you were known, the Key-Cell Cons decided whether or not you were accepted in the tank. If you were accepted by them, as I was, you would have first dibs on any available cell. If not, you were placed on the 'waiting list', which was basically 'first come first serve.' The cells within the tank held eight convicts at a time. The cells offered television along with all of the food and drugs you wanted at any time)* I was greeted by one of the guys I knew while in the Missouri State Penitentiary, and since I was immediately accepted by the Key-Cell Cons, I didn't have to pay into the poor box.

I remained in the *tank* until I went to court a couple of months later. I was sentenced to a 5010-B term *(back then that was known as a juvenile term of 4 to 6 years)* in the federal prison. After sentencing, I was sent back to the *tank* to await transfer. A few days later, United States Marshalls transported me to the Federal Prison in El Reno, Oklahoma where I was to begin my federal prison term.

I was there for only a short time when I received a visit from

Jasmine. She had apparently come to tell me that she was pregnant with my child. Needless to say, I was at a loss for words since I had heard from Bob and a couple of other friends that she had taken up with another man after I had been incarcerated. Even though I truly wanted to believe that she was carrying my child, I knew it just couldn't be true. When Jasmine explained she needed me out of prison so I could help her with the baby, I responded that I couldn't get out until I served my 4 to 6 year sentence which had basically just started. I saw the anger in her face as she abruptly terminated the visit and stormed off.

A few days later I received a letter from her letting me know that she couldn't wait for me to get out of jail, and that she was leaving me. She wrote that her mother and father were going to help her pay for a divorce and that she would be filing the papers very soon. When I read that letter, I was devastated. I thought to myself, 'Here we go again. Another person who wants to walk right out of my life.' I felt completely rejected all over again- just like how my mother had made me feel. The pain of loneliness and rejection resurfaced.

After all of these years of loneliness and isolation in a cage I, can honestly say that the worst thing that can happen to a fellow human being - child and adult alike- is rejection. I truly believe my 4 decades of pain and suffering (both physically and mentally) stem from rejection. If I didn't hear back from family or friends quick enough I immediately thought, 'Oh my God! I'm being rejected again!' Even if a guard didn't act as expected in any given situation, I became alarmed and the feeling of rejection kicked into high gear. Today, I have learned to think these things through, and try not to over react. I now sit back and evaluate the situation and wait to see the outcome as I guess any other adult would do in a "normal" situation.

Jasmine's letter put me right into "panic mode", and I convinced myself I had to get out of prison so I could be by her side. Emotionally out of control and high, (definitely a bad combination) I hit the fence and made a run for it as soon as I had the chance. I had no real hope of ever making it through the razor and barbwire and wound up cutting myself deeper with every move.

The guards fired off a warning shot over my head to let me know that the next shot would be fatal. That was enough for me to succumb to the pain of the cuts and when the guards reached me, they angrily pulled me from the tangled wires, which sliced me up even more. I was taken to the hospital where it took over 120 stitches to sew me back up. After I left the hospital, I was immediately thrown into solitary. Although the Prison Administration internally charged me with escape, which added a year in solitary confinement on to my existing prison term, they also filed charges with the Feds.

Once that case was ready to be heard, I was taken back to court where the presiding Judge tacked on an additional 5-year adult sentence. That was the first time I had ever received an adult sentence. By the time I was returned to solitary confinement (stitched up, in excruciating pain, and on the verge of divorce), I had an 11-year sentence hanging over my head. While serving my solitary sentence, I was given the opportunity to work off some of my time by busting concrete boulders into gravel. I worked for eight hours a day in the sweltering sun with a sledgehammer while being chained. Knowing that I had to get out of solitary, I didn't hesitate to take advantage of this inhumane opportunity and worked my sentence off in six months.

Similar to the State system, new arrivals to the Federal system are also put through an arduous intake process, which is commonly operated with the help of other inmates. Inmates that work in the processing building are often privy to such information like where a convict is from, and the nature of his charges. That's the very reason why certain offenders, such as sexual offenders, are immediately identified and unless they're put into protective custody upon arrival, they are usually killed within a few days of being put into general population.

Federal convicts are extremely hard-core and ruthless when compared to State inmates. Typically, they handle their business more violently and upon entering the system, instinctively become part of a *clique*. Cliques are a lot like gangs, and usually categorized by States. The stronger cliques usually lay claim to specific areas within the prison, which they unconditionally protect with their lives and perceive as their *territory*. Among the strongest and more organized cliques in my earlier days were the MM *(South American Mafia)* and the AB *(White Supremacist Brotherhood)*. These were feared adversaries against other cliques, and a simple body movement from a fellow clique member let others know who was a rival. If you weren't from the same State, you were viewed as an unwelcomed outcast or an enemy, and if you crossed their path in the wrong manner you were in eminent danger. If you were from the same State, the respective clique would size you up. Usually they'd wait to see how you handle yourself, and if you asked for protection from the other convicts. As a rule, the weakest new comers were automatically *sold-off* to rival cliques as slaves or for sexual exploitation. If for whatever reason the inmate who was *sold- off* didn't live up to his owner's desires or expectations, he'd either be killed, or put into protective custody (which is nothing more than solitary confinement) for the remainder of his sentence. Likewise, those who fought back, but were still viewed as weaklings, or were disliked for any reason, suffered an even worse fate. Those convicts who survived against all odds would literally have to sleep with a 'shank' (a prison made knife constructed from the steel of a prison bed) under their pillow, and sleep for only a few hours at a time while someone kept watch over them. They had to constantly fight other convicts and guards for respect and for the right to live.

Although fully aware of what was happening, the guards were totally indifferent to their pain and suffering. They made it perfectly clear to those in need that they wanted to go home at the end of their shift, so they were on their own. Truthfully, there's a fine line between guards and convicts. It wasn't uncommon for guards to become casualties of prison violence. They too suffered beatings, rapes and even death at the hands of convicts if they weren't able to protect themselves. Furthermore, just like convicts, the guards dealt drugs, raped, coerced the vulnerable, and even killed inmates. They were usually the first to sexually exploit the vulnerable in exchange for *temporary protection and special privileges.* Sadly, convicts who were in that situation didn't know that once they outlived their usefulness, they would suffer the worst fate of all. Typically after a guard had his fill of someone, he'd pick a clique to give the 'pigeon' to. Their owner would then pimp the convict out to other cliques for money, or sell him into slavery where it was *do or die.*

Despite coming in with an established history, I too had to prove myself in order to be accepted by both the convicts and the guards if I wanted to live and serve my sentence in general population. The only way to be accepted was to challenge someone from a rival clique, and come out the winner. If by some miracle you were victorious, the chance of you surviving until your release date was greatly improved.

The guards on the other hand, were a whole different story.

They were just as violent and skilled in 'prison politics' as the inmates were. The guards particularly enjoyed trying to break an inmate down in order to make them look weak, or soft, in the eyes of their 'home-boys'. Usually, the guards would employ what was termed *behavior modification* tactics. One of the most common methods was to use the loud speaker to call for an inmate to report to the security office, while his 'home-boys' watched. Everyone knew that you were only summoned to the security office for one of two reasons; either you were going to solitary, or you were ratting someone out.

That's why an inmate is given the 'convict rules 'upon being accepted into a clique. You are told:

1. Never speak with a guard unless you have someone from your clique with you
2. If no one is with you, always speak loud enough so that every one around you can hear the conversation
3. Always stand your ground with the guards, regardless of consequences
4. Above all, make it perfectly clear to the guards that you are just as violent as they are

As long as you followed those rules, your clique was always in the background, making their presence known to all. That was their way of publicizing their support and by showing their support publicly, both guards and convicts alike knew that going to war with you meant going to war with the entire clique.

I learned first hand that when a guard wanted to get violent with you, he would wait for his chance to catch you alone, or create the opportunity by sending several guards to handcuff and escort you back to the security office. I found myself in the latter situation shortly after being released from my solitary stint for my attempted escape.

Apparently, the guard who had ordered me sequestered had a proposition for me, which he divulged as soon as I was left alone with him. He looked me in the eyes and said, "Look KC, you're a human being, and if you join one of the cliques you'll never get out of this system. But if you help us out, we'll protect you. If things ever get bad we'll put you into protective custody so that no one can hurt you. What we'll do is call you in every now and then, making it look like you're being investigated for something and that way none of the cliques will suspect that you're working for us." He quickly followed his spiel by asking me, "How does that sound to you KC?"

I took great pleasure in letting that guard know that his proposition wasn't going to be considered by me for even one second. I calmly reminded the guard that I had spent most of my childhood in correctional institutions and have had everything taken away from me by people just like him. They were people who didn't care about me, but instead only cared about fulfilling their own personal agenda at my expense. Needless to say my official response to his offer was, "You have a hell of a nerve asking me to help you harm a fellow convict while you keep me locked up in a cage for years!" He replied by asking me, "Which do you think is better Amos, never getting out of prison, or being killed?"

I said, "Look, I don't have anything else to say to you. Just know that I would rather take my chances in the world that you people have kept me in since I was a child, than snitch anyone out."

Unsurprisingly, he wasn't very happy with my perspective on the whole deal and angrily said, "Alright. You're going to have to learn the hard way. We gave you an opportunity to make things right for yourself and you blew it. You've made your bed, and now you have to sleep in it, Convict!"

Some time had passed since that day, and one of the guards who had escorted me to the security office back then, was now escorting me to solitary for an alleged stabbing. As he was walking me towards the solitary cell he says, "You know KC, we wouldn't have respected you if you had become a "stool pigeon" for us way back then. You did exactly what I would have done to prove that I was a man."

It took all of two seconds for me to differentiate him from me. I told him, "You're not a man to be respected. You're an institutionalized guard who uses human beings to move up in rank, just like the convicts do. You're more pathetic than the convicts though because you've helped to destroy any human decency that they once had. Unlike you, they've actually earned this 'sick' type of respect that you crave in this hellhole. Man, all you guards are the same. You force us to live this life and never stop trying to break us down." Then I asked, "What is it that you people are hoping to accomplish by breaking us down? I mean, what are you breaking us down to become?"

Being that I was already in the hole, I let loose and told him straight up, "You guards make me sick! You are the institutionalized ones, not me! I have cause for my actions because I'm just trying to survive in order to get out of this situation so that I may someday live a *normal* life. Unlike you and your kind who will always be stuck in this man-made madness, I want to get out of this situation that I've been put into against my will. And remember this; you're kidding yourself if you or any of the other guards thinks that you guys are in charge. The truth of the matter is that you're only running what the convicts allow you to run."

By now, I had made him so mad that he pushed me into the cell and slammed the gate shut. As I turned back to look at him, I laughed and shrugged my shoulders. He on the other hand, just stood on the other side of the gate looking at me for the longest time without saying a word. I could tell that he knew what I had just told him about prison was true. As the saying goes, "If looks could kill, I'd be dead'. *After that day he never directed another word toward me, and went out of his way to not even make eye contact.*

As it turns out, the guy in the solitary cell next to mine (a fella out of St. Louis, Missouri who went by the name of Bones) overheard everything that I told the guard, and as soon as the guard left he called out to me. I'll never forget his words - he said, "KC, you sure told that pig off. Man, I want you to know that you have my respect."

I responded by saying, "Is that right?" He said, "It sure is. That's why I'm in solitary now because we have to earn our respect."

Curiously I asked him, "And how did you do that, Bones?"

He said, "Well, this home-boy from St. Louis wanted the cell next to mine back in the cell block, but this other cat was next in line for that same cell. So, out of respect, I asked him if I could buy the cell from him so that my home-boy could move in next to me. The dude totally insulted me by saying that the cell wasn't open because he lived there now. Since I didn't want to get ugly with the guy right then and there, I told him 'all right', and I left. But in the back of my mind I told myself, 'alright dude... then I'll just have to move you'."

As Bones started laughing he said, "Well, you know what I mean KC."

I responded, "No, Bones, I don't."

"Well I'll tell you what I did. I waited until he was asleep, and I killed him. And to get my respect, I cut out his heart and hung it outside the window by a string. I didn't think that one through because now no one is in that cell, and I'm in the hole facing either a life sentence or the death penalty." Indifferently he asked "So, what do you think about that, KC?"

A bit shocked by his bluntness I said, "Bones, you're a sick dude."

He then asked, "You think so, KC?" I quickly replied, "You know it, man."

After that conversation, all I could do was sit there and think about the sick sense of respect that these convicts crave within these human warehouses. Still to this day, the thought of it makes me sick to my stomach. For the life of me I can't understand why most of the guys in prison, especially the smart ones, can't figure out that the penal system that they have been thrown into is destroying their mind and all human decency in the bogus name of 'respect'. For those who are unfamiliar with the United States Correctional system, it's a government sanctioned human repository for those deemed substandard by society. A structure that forces people to live in such deplorable conditions that for most, as I'm sure was the case with Bones, self perseverance can only be attained by devaluing the lives of others. Just in case you've ever wondered why so many 'rehabilitated' convicts come out worse than when they went in - that's why.

Personally, I know that the penal system is nothing more than a moneymaker under the guise of 'rehabilitation' and 'human services.' It's a system that typically pays convicts approximately $1.50 per day and then forces them to buy everything, including toilet paper from their store (referred to as the 'canteen').

After serving unjustified time in solitary confinement, I was officially cleared of all the trumped up charges that landed me there.

Once settled back into general population, a hardcore prison killer bent on earning his prison respect, named Duke, approached me. *Duke is synonymous with trouble. All he cared about was beating or raping people, and I viewed him as a real sick dude. I didn't like him from the start, but the home-boys accepted him and respected his demented ways. I guess that's probably because they were no different. Unlike all of them, I despised bullies and violence in general. I only joined their ranks to increase my chances of surviving this man- made hell until my release. Duke is a quintessential example of the penal system 's 'Behavior Modification' program, which is funded by your tax dollars.*

One day he was standing in front of me said, "KC, I don't like you. When I get the chance to kill you, I'm gonna take it." *As we stood there staring at each other, all that came to mind was that this dude must really be high on something because murderers like him don't warn their victims about what's going to happen to them. They just don't 'tip their hat' in this situation. That's just not how it's done in the penal jungle. While I actually appreciated the fact that he, for whatever reason warned me of his intentions, I knew that I had to make my move on him first.*

I simply responded, "Duke, I don't have a personal beef with you, but the truth is, I never really liked you, or your ways."

Apparently shocked by my bluntness he asked, "What did you say?"

"I said what I said Duke," I replied. By now I could see the anger in his eyes, and that the veins in his neck were bulging. "You can't disrespect the Brotherhood like that!" he yelled.

I calmly responded, "Duke, I'm not disrespecting the Brotherhood- I'm disrespecting YOUR sorry ass."

Totally chomped by my unintimidated attitude, he looked at

me real hard and through his clenched teeth he muttered, "It's on KC. You're a dead man."

"Bring it, Duke", I sneered, and although we stepped off and went our separate ways, it was clear to both of us what came next. Like with most cowards, Duke couldn't backup his threat by himself, so he ran back to the brotherhood and told them I had disrespected them.

A couple of days later they approached me during work detail and said, "We hear you don't have any respect for us."

Not wanting to get into a confrontation with the entire Brotherhood I quickly replied, "No, I didn't say anything to that affect. As a matter of fact, I specifically told Duke to his face that my lack of respect was for him personally and NOT the brotherhood. This whole thing has absolutely nothing to do with you guys. Duke was the one who brought the war to my door, I just welcomed it."

After what I had told them sunk in, they asked, "Is that the way it went down, KC?"

I replied affirmatively.

They then said, "Alright, we'll stay out of this and it'll be a one-on-one as long as you don't involve any of your home boys."

Shrugging my shoulders I replied, "That's fine by me. I've always fought my own wars- win or lose."

As they all walked away, I knew not to count on their word because the rules of the game are 10 for 1. That simply meant that if you hurt one of their home-boys, then they would hurt 10 of yours. As soon as I finished work, I went back to my unit to warn my home-boys of what just went down with the Brotherhood. Although they agreed that it would be a one-on-one, they didn't hesitate to say, "Hey KC, if the Brotherhood wants war, then war it will be."

I told them, "No. It's not between them and us; it's between

107

me and Duke."

Days went by and since everyone knew that war was waging between Duke and I, the tension was felt throughout the entire unit. Even the guards made comments like, "We hope you two animals kill each other off."

As the days became weeks, my guard heightened, and I became extremely cautious when turning corners. I knew that Duke was doing the same and that we were both packing shanks. *(I kept mine tucked between my waistband and lower back just incase I was forced into an unfair fight against more than one convict.)* Unbelievably, I had home-boys from both cliques *(his and mine)* giving me the 'low down' that Duke was talking about making his move on me anytime now. Even though I feared the outcome, I wanted to bring this whole thing to an end quickly.

As expected, one particular afternoon set the stage. As soon as I got off from work, I returned to my cellblock. On this day however, as I was walking towards the cellblock door I noticed several convicts I had never seen before hanging around outside and going into the cellblock. I knew at that moment that it was about to go down between Duke and I, and that the waiting was finally coming to an end.

In anticipation of this day, I used my canteen items to pay a couple of convicts that specialized in making war weapons (that's how they supported themselves) to make me some upper body armor. They made this armor by gluing old magazines together for added strength, and sewing prison issued army-style belts around them so that I could strap the armor onto my abdominal and upper chest area. This would help protect me from receiving deep stab wounds.

Wearing my armor under my clothes and having my shank concealed by my coat, I felt my adrenalin running high. I entered the cellblock and as I'm turning the corner... BAM!!!

Duke shoved his shank into my abdominal area, but because of my armor it only went in about an inch and got stuck. As he was trying to pull his shank out, I slammed down on the back of his neck with my shank. When he was finally able to free his shank, he lunged at me and stabbed me in the left shoulder. Since I had no protection up there, the shank went in about three inches deep and the blood immediately started gushing from my shoulder. I struck him again, landing my shank in his chest. By now there's blood everywhere, and I could hear the other convicts yelling, "Duke's down!"

As I looked to my side I saw the guards running towards me yelling, "Everybody get out of the way!" But before they arrived, my home-boys ran up and encircled me. Duke's did the same. *It was a surreal situation, like a stand off that you see in the movies.* The home-boys on both sides took the shanks from us and handed them off to other convicts so the guards wouldn't have any evidence against either one of us. By the time the guards reached us, the shanks were gone and they told everyone to get back into their cell.

Seeing Duke still on the floor holding his chest and in a fetal position, the Sergeant called out to one of the guards to get on his radio and to call the infirmary. "Tell them to get a team down to C-block right away! There is a convict down!"

He walked over and although I was bleeding profusely, he hand cuffed me and asked, "Where are the shanks?"

Instinctively, I replied, "What shanks?"

He yanked my left arm and said, "Alright, smart ass."

At that moment the nurse arrived with two helpers, and a stretcher. As they were getting Duke up off the floor and putting him on the stretcher, he looked over at me and said, "You're dead, KC."

109

Once on the stretcher, the nurse quickly examined him and told the sergeant that Duke needed to be transferred to an outside facility because the infirmary wasn't equipped to care for him. She told him that security would have to clear his transfer immediately or that Duke would die.

The Sergeant told her that he would go to the Administration Building to authorize the transfer while she stayed with Duke, and told another guard to walk me to the infirmary to have my shoulder checked out. When I got there, the nurse asked me where I had been stabbed. I told her that I had been hit in the shoulder, to which she replied "Please take off your coat and shirt so I may have a look." Clearly, she was stunned to see my prison made body armor, and in awe she said to the guard, "Will you look at this!"

Stunned himself the guard asked me, "What is that?"

Since I wouldn't say a word, he just started taking pictures of my stab wounds, the blood, and my armor. The nurse told the guard that I needed at least seven stitches to close up my wounds, and she started to stitch me up.

Once the guard finished taking pictures, he said to the nurse "I've never seen anything like this vest in all the years I've been here. Wait until Security sees this. They'll want to send this to our training facility for our new officers."

The guard then said to me, "Well I'll be damned Amos. You were definitely ready for battle boy. Old Duke sure did underestimate you!" As soon as the nurse finished with me, the guard told her that he was taking me straight to solitary for questioning. On the way walking there he said, "Amos, I'm sure you'll be charged for this, and you better hope Duke doesn't die. You know the Federal System recently enacted the Death Penalty for inmates who kill other inmates." With my mouth still shut, I was placed into solitary.

That evening a FBI agent from the local unit came to interview me and asked me about the shanks. "What shanks?" I replied.

"The one Duke stabbed you with, and the one we know you had. Un-phased, I told him that I didn't know anything about a shank, and that I had no idea how Duke or I were wounded. He came back at me with, "So you want to play hard ball, huh Amos? Well, if Duke dies we'll see to it that you get the death penalty, but if he lives and you work with us to get rid of this guy, we'll see what we can do to help you out. Believe me; we know all about both of you, and Duke's background makes you look like a choirboy."

Knowing that he was just blowing smoke up my ass, I expressed to him again that I didn't know anything and that he didn't have a shank to use as evidence against me. So unless he was charging me with stabbing myself and eating the shank, I just wanted to go back to my cell so that I could lie down because I was starting to feel light-headed after loosing so much blood.

Obviously the FBI agent wasn't going to let it go and sarcastically said, "Well, I guess you're blind, and a shank just flew out of nowhere and hit you at the very same time that Duke suddenly dropped to the floor with a hole in his chest. Right?"

Calmly, I replied, "Once again, I don't know anything, and more importantly, you don't know anything. Why don't you go grill Duke about what happened to him?"

Obviously mad at my uncaring attitude, he told me that I wasn't going to go back to my cell, but that instead I was gonna rot in solitary and that I'd better hope that Duke survived. He then told the guard that was with us to put me into solitary indefinitely.

Six months passed since the incident with Duke. I was still in

111

solitary confinement awaiting the FBI's decision as to whether or not I'd be charged for self-defense. Through the grapevine I learned that Duke survived, and that he had been transferred back to the infirmary. After a week in the infirmary, he was sent to another solitary unit and was also waiting on a decision from the FBI. I overheard a guard say that because we were considered a danger to each other, we would have to be separated while incarcerated. This meant that once the FBI decided our fate, one of us would probably be transferred to another prison.

Ironically, some of my home-boys worked in the same solitary unit where Duke was being housed. I guess Duke was still running his mouth about killing me, and they wanted to know if I wanted him 'taken out' (which meant killed), but I told them no. They pushed the issue by reminding me that he might turn over on me, and tell the Feds that I was the one who shanked him. I assured them that Duke wasn't going to roll on me because he knew that if he did, he'd have to serve the rest of his time in solitary. Besides, the Feds really didn't have a case against either one of us because they didn't have any weapons or witnesses. Satisfied, my home-boys said, "Alright, KC. We'll respect your decision."

After a few more weeks in solitary, I was told that the FBI finally decided to officially abandon their investigation due to the lack of evidence, and that I was to be transferred to a high-level security facility because of my involvement.

Chapter 12

Ashland, KY

The guard who was on duty in solitary at the time told me that the new facility I was heading to was *escape proof.* He told me the prison was equipped with laser beam alarms that instantly went off if anyone got within 15 feet of either side of the perimeter fence. He also told me there were off-road Jeeps at each corner of the prison that were equipped with a computerized map of the entire facility which allowed them to accurately pinpoint any security breach and alert the guards by highlighting the breached area instantly. Apparently taking great joy in his spiel, the guard made it a point to also inform me that if by some miracle someone actually made it to the fence, it was 'shoot to kill' at that point. He then started laughing and told me that I'd never get out of there because the director of the Federal Bureau of Prisons had the Ashland, Kentucky facility built just for me. As he walked away he added that the *boys* running that prison would change my ways for sure.

A few days later I was woken at 4 o'clock in the morning and told I was being transferred to another facility. Remembering what I had been told by the guard about Ashland, I asked where I was going.

Ignoring my request for confirmation as to where I would be sent, the guards opened my cell door, searched me, gave me a change of clothes and chained me up. (Only this time they immobilized my hands by placing a special device-basically a 3"x5" black box- over the chain between the cuffs.) They then walked me into the prison bus which already had about 32 convicts seated and chained to the floor. The bus drove us to the local airport where we would be flown courtesy of ConAir (short for 'Convict Airline' - the penal system's privately owned prison transport) to our next destination.

When we arrived at the airport we were loaded into a 727 and just like on the bus, we were seated and chained to the floor. This was the quickest way to transfer convicts between multiple facilities and once we arrived at the 'lay over' facility, we were loaded back onto a prison bus and driven the rest of the way to our final destination.

When I arrived at Ashland, I could immediately tell that it was a brand new facility. It was big, intimidating, and I truly believe this prison was built with the intentions of instilling fear from the moment you laid eyes on it. Usually upon arriving at a new prison, the first thing I did was to start scoping out any possible means of escape, but just like opening a Christmas present, the excitement of what was in the box was gone quickly.

As soon as the guards boarded the bus they started calling out names and numbers, and you actually had to respond verbally by saying, "I'm here," or "that's me," when you heard your name. *Perhaps they thought you could just chew the chains off and disappear through the walls of the bus without the countless guards noticing.*

Once head count was cleared, the welcome spiel started. "Most of you have been shipped to Ashland because you think that rules don't apply to you. Well, let me tell all of you convicts that here, you WILL follow the rules. You won't be able to even blink without us letting you, and if any of you think that's bullshit, you'll

114

soon learn that it's not. This facility was built for those who need to have their thinking corrected. Also, if anyone here even thinks for one second that you can escape- you're dead wrong.

Ashland was built with a state-of-the-art security system and if for some reason the system goes down and you're able to get around it, you'll be fatally shot on the spot. As part of your processing, you will be assigned housing and a job assignment, and now that you have officially been welcomed, you'll unload the bus in a straight and silent line."

I equate arriving at another prison to being the star attraction at a freak show. All the ticket holders are anxiously lined up all over the place waiting to see who you are. They scrutinize you as they try to determine whether or not sometime in their miserable lives your paths have crossed before. For some, the site of a familiar face (especially a friendly one) would somehow help them move through the next day in hell. I myself have been recognized and greeted in numerous prisons by other convicts who usually yell out the same thing wherever I go, "Yo! That's KC," and "This joint can't hold him. That dude moves swiftly and takes care of business silently." They'd usually yell out, "Hey KC, whaz up!" like we were tight or something. Hell, half of them I never even spoke to, although we probably bunked in the same unit. Usually right after being greeted by the convicts, the guards would chime in as well with, "You see that one there. His name is Amos, but he goes by KC. He's not to be trusted. Let me tell ya 'bout ol KC. He's hospitalized several convicts and guards alike at every place he's been at, so keep your eyes on him from a distance. Don't go near him by yourself if he's fighting because he'll beat you down as well. Call for back up before you approach him, then make sure you beat the hell outta him." And just like the convicts, they also acknowledged my

115

presence by asking how I was doing as I walked by. However, the strange thing about their recognition was that unlike some of the convicts who actually knew me, most of them solely based their opinion of me off of stories from convicts or other guards.

After processing, the freak show started all over again as cellblocks were assigned. This time you get guys asking, "Whatcha do this time, KC?" or commenting, "Man, you're not going to like it here in this hell hole." *Yeah, as if I liked it in any other prison.* When I heard those comments all I thought to myself was that those guys didn't think before they opened their mouth, so I'd just keep walking.

As they were checking me out, I scanned the room for the convicts who liked to 'scope out' the naive, vulnerable, potential moneymaker, or outstanding hit that they could capitalize on for someone else. By the time I finally reached my cell, I was exhausted from all the greetings that I had to deal with, along with my new *bunky* who had been used to living alone in an 8' x 12' cage all by himself. Being forced to live with another man in such a small space for 24 hours a day is horrendous, to say the least. As the new 'meat', you're at a disadvantage right from the start. Not only does each of you have to figure out the other's demeanor, but since he arrived first, he believes that the cage belongs to him and that you have to follow his rules. If the new bunky hasn't been institutionalized, he'll quickly acknowledge that the cage doesn't belong to anyone, that you're both there to do your time, and that you'll need to just meet at the halfway mark to get along while you have to. On the other hand if you're paired up with someone who's hardcore and a product of the system, he'll see you as the enemy who's trying to move into his space. There's only one way to handle that type of bunky and it involves closing the cell door and fighting until he accepts that the cage doesn't belong to just him. In either case, once mutual respect has been established you can begin to figure out what you'll need to do in order to accomplish your goals while in the midst of total madness.

I spent my first 5 months at Ashland discreetly analyzing the entire compound from top to bottom and hadn't found a possible way out. Then out of the blue, I was approached by a convict who told me that it had been rumored that an additional cellblock was built outside the main compound adjacent to the Administrative Building. The cellblock was built with the intentions of housing only those inmates deemed obedient, and was referred to as the *honor unit*. Since anyone housed in the *honor unit* received special privileges, it seemed that you could easily escape. The only way in however, was by earning a transfer. He flat out told me that anyone who had ever escaped, or attempted to escape from a previous prison would never be allowed to live there because it was too close to freedom and security was so relaxed. After hearing him out, all that I focused on was the part about having to *earn* your transfer into the *honor unit*, rather than not being eligible if you had attempted an escape before.

Wait a minute, I told myself. What kind of rule is that? Here I've been, imprisoned since I was 10 just because my mother didn't want the responsibility of taking care of me. I've become a quintessential product of the United States Juvenile system, which shoved me right into the Adult Correctional system where I have been forced to live with hardened criminals from an early age. I want to be part of the land of the free! I want to evoke my rights to make my own decisions and voice my own opinions! And because I've had to protect myself from abuse by trying to escape this vile environment, you're telling me that I'm not even eligible to be 'considered' for the honor unit? That was a devastating moment in my life. I essentially realized that I was destined to stay in the pits of

117

hell for the rest of my life. There was no doubt in my mind that I bore
some type of mark signifying "rejection." All of my life to that point I
had been forced into situations based on rejection. There was
absolutely no doubt in my mind that anyone's life could be this
miserable. I thought that this all must be a nightmare and that I
would eventually wake up.

A couple of days passed and as I sat in the mess hall with the
guy who told me about the *honor unit,* I noticed that a certain door
was being used by those convicts only. Out of curiosity, I asked the
guy I was sitting with what he thought would happen if I just got up
and walked out that door with the rest of them?

Clearly taken back by what I just asked, he replied, "I don't
know, man. What are you going to do?" I simply told him that I was
going to give it a try, and that if there's any way out of this hell-hole,
it's got to be beyond that door.

Shaking his head he said, "KC, you never give up, do you?"

I didn't hesitate a second to respond, "Why should I, man? I
have to try and get out of here using anyway that I can." Nearly in a
whisper, he wished me well and all the luck in the world. In a
similarly low voice I told him that it's not luck I was looking
forward to- it was my right to be free. I also added that I had to make
my move right now. I would never get the chance to be transferred to
the *honor unit*, and I can't continue to sit in a cage year after year.

I told him earlier I was walking the yard with another
convict, and listening to what he was telling me. He told me about all
that he had before he came in, and how he will have nothing left
when he gets out. It was torture listening to that. I conveyed to him
that the day you believe that you're never going to get out of prison
is the last day of your life. When you settle for just walking the
prison yard, you begin to live in a fantasy world. I also told him I

118

truly believe there are rules and regulations that must be followed to balance the rights and wrongs of everyday life, and that those who commit a crime run the risk of getting caught, and possibly paying a price for their misdeed. Those people who try to cheat the system often wind up paying the piper either way and are not only judged by the so called 'justice' system, but by other convicts as well.

Nodding his head in agreement, he told me that he saw my point and that if more cons thought like me, they couldn't hold us in there. As he chuckled, I shook my head and told him that it wasn't funny; it was the truth.

As we parted ways it occurred to me that the convict that I was talking to couldn't relate to my quest for freedom because he was sentenced to life in prison without parole. He allowed the system to institutionalize him and accepted the fact that he would live out his days in a cage. The yearning for freedom no longer existed within him, and apparently hadn't for some time now. I wouldn't allow that to happen to me.

A few days later during supper, I made up my mind. I knew that I couldn't wait any longer and that I had to go through that door to see what my chances were on the other side. After eating, I got up and followed the *honor block* convicts right out of the door. I didn't notice any eyes on me, which implied that there was a flaw in the security. The guards were indeed extremely relaxed when it came to the *honor block* convicts. Although my heart was pounding so hard that it felt like it was about to burst, I was able to focus on my surroundings.

Despite the darkness, I could clearly see the Administrative Building in the distance, as well as the drainpipes on the side of the building, which ran from top to bottom. Seeing those pipes brought an incredible sense of joy. I knew that if I ran as fast as I could from

119

the *honor block* to the Administrative Building and jumped over the ground beam alarm, I could use the drainpipes to climb to the roof. I could then jump down from the roof, and head towards the woods. That's exactly what I did.

As soon as I got to the roof, I noticed a *trip wire* that ran across the entire length of the building. I simply stepped over it, and listened for the sounds of running guards or fast moving vehicles. After two or three minutes of silence I knew that I had beaten the alarm system and was on the brink of freedom. Once in the woods, I ran as far and as fast as I could. I continued to walk throughout the entire night. As soon as morning hit, I could see Ashland's Jeeps and plenty of State Troopers speeding along the edge of the woods, along with a helicopter hovering above. I knew they were looking for me, so I hid under some thick brush. I soon heard barking, and knew that it was just a matter of time before the dogs sniffed me out.

Hanging on to false hope I thought that if I laid still enough, the dogs would just keep going. Eventually though, the dogs had me surrounded. Guards and troopers were all around me with their guns and rifles drawn. Even though I couldn't see who was saying what, I heard one of them say, "Come on Amos, give us a reason to blow your head off," and another one said, "We should just kill you anyway."

Initially I thought, 'Go ahead - I'd be better off dead'. But then I thought, 'No. There 's always another day and maybe next time I'll be able to make it to freedom.'

As the guards brought me back to prison, I could see that they were tickled pink. One would think that they had won the Olympics, and that they were going to receive a gold medal for their deed. When I made it back to Ashland, the guard on duty told those escorting me that the Warden had ordered I be taken to the Security Office so he could personally question me. Immediately upon his arrival to the Security Office, the Warden asked me how I got out of his prison. My mind started scrambling for a response since it was obvious they hadn't figured out the *honor block* connection. I figured if I didn't tell him the truth, maybe I could use that same tactic again someday. I instead told him I had escaped by climbing the fences. Angrily he slammed his fist against the wall and yelled, "No! No! You didn't climb my fences because none of the alarms went off!"

Unimpressed with his anger I replied, "Warden, what can I say. I went over your fences. Believe it or not sir, that's how I escaped."

My refusal to change my story only infuriated him more and as his veins bulged on the side of his neck he yelled, "I'm charging you with escape and adding another 5 years to your sentence!" He told the guards to take me to solitary and to have someone posted outside of my cell 24 hours a day until I went to court and was subsequently transferred out of his prison.

After addressing the guards, he readdressed me by telling me that this was my last chance. If I worked with him and told him how I had escaped from his prison without setting off any of the alarms, he'd see what he could do to get me a lesser sentence. Not budging from my story, I told him that I had already let him know how I got out. At that point, he ordered the guards to take me away.

As I was being shackled for the walk from the Administrative Building to solitary, I overheard the Warden telling the Assistant Warden that the BOP was going to want some answers as to how a convict with a prior escape record was able to get out of a top security prison without setting off any of the alarms. The Warden also told him that he knew his boss was going to retire him over the escape. Clearly enraged, he addressed me once more by saying, "Don't think that for one second I believe you Amos. I'm going to find out how you got out of here. Believe you me, you can bet your ass on that one!"

Although at that moment I realized I would probably never get another chance to use my escape plan, I figured I could at least pass it on to another convict and give someone else the chance to obtain their freedom. And I did!

A couple of days passed when some hot shots from Washington, D.C. showed up to interview me. They questioned me as to how I was able to get out of Ashland and were making all kinds of promises about a lesser, or no additional sentence if I cooperated with them by telling the truth. Refusing to stray from my original story, I told them the same thing that I had told the Warden. I had climbed the fences. As with the Warden, they too were angry by the time they were finished questioning me.

I finally went to court two weeks later, and was informed by my lawyer at the time that the BOP had a witness against me that could outline my escape scheme.

Well, that just completely blew my defense since I was planning on informing the court that I hadn't escaped. My plan was to tell them that Ashland had opened the front gate and released me. I figured what the heck- it's their word against mine! How can someone like me successfully escape from such a top security prison without setting off a single alarm?

Once again, it turned out that a convict used the *system* for personal gain. If given the chance, even the tightest lipped convict would seize the opportunity to be freed from the pits of hell, even if just temporarily. As I'm sure you've figured out, the guy who told me about the *honor block* was the same one who ratted me out to the Feds. He did it in exchange for a transfer to an outside prison camp. After all was said and done, I had five years added to my existing term and sentenced to an additional year in solitary. I was transferred out of Ashland to the FCI (Federal Correctional Institute) Petersburg Prison Complex in Petersburg, Virginia.

Chapter 13

Petersburg, VA

Since I was now being transferred to a 'Super Max' facility, I was guarded like an endangered animal at the zoo. Despite the special treatment, I was still able to scope out the joint. Disappointingly, the only way out of that place was to run and hit the fence, which undoubtedly meant certain death. A friend of mine, Poe, tried that route and was fatally shot right off of the fence.

While in Virginia, I quickly accepted the fact that I was not always going to be able accomplish my goal. Certain situations arise that prevent us from altering the path that we must take on our journey in this life. I learned the hard way that my determination to find short-cuts had always left me worse off than if I had just followed the path I was suppose to in the first place. Since my actions never got me any closer to my goal, I accepted the fact that I had to wait until it was my turn to move forward.

Upon completion of my orientation period at Petersburg, I was released from solitary into general population. Day after day I hoped that I would find a way out of there, until eventually I ran into some trouble with one of the guards. There was this convict named Elijah that I had befriended, and I decided that I was going to help him get through his short, three-year sentence. Although it was his first time being incarcerated, he stepped up to the plate, and fought back when it was necessary to do so. He didn't have a prison mentality though, and he was scared to death of it in there due to the stabbings and clique wars that became a way of life. One afternoon, Elijah and I were walking from the cellblock to the yard to pump some iron *(I've lifted weights off and on for a few reasons, including for my health, but mainly to stay strong)*. This particular guard, who was always looking for trouble, was sitting behind his desk in his reclining chair waiting for someone to harass. As luck would have it- it was our turn. As we passed him he yelled out, "Where you going, convicts?"

Hoping to avoid any conflict I quickly replied, "We're headed to the yard."

Of course, being the guard that he was, he looked towards Elijah and said, "What about you punk? Where do you think you're going?"

I immediately saw the fear in Elijah's eyes, so I turned and said to the guard, "Look, this guy's not used to prison, so why don't you just give him a break." Boy, did my good intentions annoy the guard!

Now sitting up in his chair he said, "Who the hell are you to speak up for him? Are you his daddy?"

Calmly I responded, "Look man, you're always messing with people. Don't you have anything better to do than to mess with us?"

Totally outraged by my boldness he yelled, "What did you say!!!"

I replied, "I said - leave this guy alone, he's not causing you any trouble."

Peeved beyond belief, he told me the only one who talks to him like that was his old man. The guard's face was now as red as a tomato, and I knew he had no intentions of letting the whole situation go. I told him that if he was looking for trouble, he'd better mess with me and leave Elijah out of it. No sooner had I finished my sentence that I realized that my anger had got the best of me. I had gone too far with that guard. He made a quick move to get up out of his chair and as soon as I saw him standing, I hit him. I ended up hitting him so hard that when I knocked him back into his chair, the chair went flying backwards and the guard hit the floor. As soon as he got his wind back, he jumped up and triggered the alarm.

I told Elijah to get out of there because a bunch of guards would be 'bum rushing' to the scene any second. He made it out of the area just in time, and as I saw about 12 guards running up on me for the kill, I asked another convict that had been standing nearby to look out for Elijah for me. The convict didn't hesitate for a second to say, "You got it, KC."

Of course being the honorable person that he was, the trouble making guard told the others that I had assaulted him in his chair for absolutely no reason. He told them that he was just sitting there minding his own business when I just came up on him outta the blue and hit him.

The 'Kill Squad' gladly slammed me against the wall face first, and tried to break my arms while they were cuffing me so that they could haul me off to solitary. Since no one can attest to what happens while in a solitary cell, they took turns beating me until I blacked out. When I finally regained consciousness, I was so badly beaten that I couldn't get up from the floor for three days. As soon as I was able to crawl to the bed, I was informed that I would be charged with assaulting a guard. This of course meant that I would face outside charges carrying an additional 5 to 10 year sentence. The additional time would be added onto my existing sentence, as opposed to running parallel with my current sentence.

By now I had so much time added to my original sentence that I couldn't keep it straight anymore. It got to the point where I realized that my life didn't matter to the people running these correctional facilities. It seemed that all they wanted was to keep me locked up for the rest of my life so they could exploit my labor, and anything else they could get out of me. As the days, weeks, months, and years went by I grew angrier and angrier with the *system.* I not only hated the guards, but also the other convicts that were bent on harming fellow inmates. My hatred was so strong that it became physically visible, and caused my stomach acid to rise up and run out of the corners of my mouth. This caused cracking and bleeding. At first I thought that I had a severe case of heartburn, but then I started to think that the guards were putting something in my food. A few days later, I dropped a slip *(submitted a request form)* to see a doctor. To my surprise, he told me that I was causing my own health problems. Not having a clue about what he was referring to I asked, "Whatta ya mean, doc?"

He replied, "Listen Amos, you're so angry and full of hatred that your body is producing large amounts of stomach acid. The only way the acid can escape is through your mouth- similar to a rabid dog. If you don't try to relax and alleviate your stress, you're going to kill yourself."

Dumbfounded, I said, "I hear ya doc, but just give me something for my heartburn, please." He gave me a handful of antacids and sent me on my way.

When I got back to my cell I laid in my bunk and thought, 'Man! That doctor is full of crap. He's no different than the rest of the staff in the *system.* He's trained to make us think that all of our illnesses are nothing but a figment of our imagination'. I truly believed that this was a tactic used against us so we'd shut down and no longer fight for ourselves. To prove that I was right about him, I decided to try really hard to relax. Well wouldn't you know it- within

127

a few days I was feeling better. The sores around my mouth were starting to heal, and the burning sensation had become much better. It was only when I became angry that the acid returned; that's when I knew it was time to cool out.

Because of the assault on the guard, I was forced to live in solitary within an isolated cellblock that was used to house those who are considered to be 'anti-system thinkers.' In other words, anti system thinkers were those whom the system considered a threat to their authority, and who were afraid would initiate a movement against them. Even though I didn't know any of convicts in there, as soon as they heard about my past, one would have thought they all knew me. I really wasn't interested in what they had to say, nor did I want to hear about their beliefs. I had enough to worry about with my own attitude, and convicts like them were usually nothing more than 'wanna be's'. I knew that I didn't fit in with their faction, because they didn't have the knowledge or the heart to be what they claimed to be.

One day, the so-called 'leader' of the bunch called out to me and asked what I thought about what he had been saying.

Offhandedly, I replied, "Well, I certainly could have done without it and quite frankly, I'm not impressed at all by what I have heard."

Shocked, he asked, "What did you just say, man?"

Now totally annoyed because he was cutting into my reading time, I told him that I couldn't care less about what he and the rest of his boys had to say, especially since what I was witnessing was nothing but a whole lot of talk and no action. I went on to say that he was the one calling me out, trying to convince me to share his viewpoint. I also told him that everything's fine, and he can keep talking all that gobbledygook, but trying to recruit me was a waste of time.

Clearly insulted by my candor, he had the audacity to ask if I was looking for some action. Trying my hardest not to bust out laughing I replied, "See man! That's exactly what I'm talking about- all talk and no action. You know damned well that there's no human contact here and that we'll never be out at the same time to finish this conversation. So just shut up until you can put up."

I could hear his cronies laughing harder than me, knowing that he just got punked. All that he could come back with was, "Alright! Alright! It's on the first chance we get!"

Unmoved by his senseless threat, I replied, "Yeah, yeah, yeah. If that is the one thought that's going to get you through the day, then fine- the first chance we get, its on." Unsurprisingly, none of us ever talked to each other again.

Thinking back about all those guys, I truly believe that they never really had anything of importance in their life, or anything that they could claim as their own. Before they came to prison they probably didn't have any beliefs or ambitions. And since they seemed to not have much heart in their quest, they almost certainly never achieved any sort of goal in their lifetimes. That's why when they came to prison, they found themselves without a purpose, so they had to seek out others who were in the same boat. They are the ones who when thrown into prison, yearn to become somebody that will be respected by those who share a similar life, or have similar beliefs. It's in prison that they thrive on the thought of becoming somebody, and even though they find it easy to achieve their 'jailhouse' respect within a group, they don't understand that there's a price to pay for all the bullying they've inflicted. They don't understand that you must have a heart to hang on to your respect because when you're imprisoned, every other convict wants what you have. It's quite sad

*that so many of the guys that I have come across over the years only
live for the moment, and can't see past that second in time. They
can't figure out that once that moment passes, they have nothing
else. It's no different than 'the box' syndrome that so many people
live in on the outside. Regrettably, people on the outside become so
complacent and content with just what's in their 'box' that they never
strive to climb out of it to see what else life has to offer them. I told
many guys to try thinking out of their box, but they quickly became
angry with me because I wasn't falling for their mumbo-jumbo life
style. I had a different opinion, and they just didn't want to hear it.
They're the people faking themselves out, and the fact that I wasn't a
generic convict didn't sit well with them. Although I had absolutely
no problem with them doing their own thing- hell, it was their life - I
strongly believe that the penal system is thrilled when there are
convicts eager to remain dumber than a box of rocks and who are
easy to mold.*

*It's a much different story when the system spots a convict
that can think on his own, reason, and actually see the picture for
what it is. Warning flags start going up. Immediately all kinds of
notations are made to one's file so that everyone in the system is
aware that they're not dealing with a dummy. Instead, they are
warned that they're dealing with someone smart who can see
through the smoke screens, so caution must be used when dealing
with this type of prisoner. To them, the most dangerous convict isn't
the murderer, but instead the one with a brain who can logically
think for himself. Their biggest fear is that you may decide to form a
faction and begin to educate other convicts. You're instantly
portrayed as a threat to not only the system, but to the general
population.*

The system's main objective now shifts from overseer, to

oppressor as they try to shut you down by using any means necessary. The system becomes consumed with the notion that they must keep you, and any one like you, locked away in solitary for as long as possible. Their mission is to eliminate any contact with other convicts that may become conscious of what's going on. Not only is an intuitive convict a threat to the control of the prison, but more importantly he's a threat to their job security!

While I was sitting there in solitary, I often thought to myself that when the day comes, I would welcome the opportunity to enlighten the public about the things that go on beyond the gates and behind the cell doors. But then I'd wonder if anyone would believe me. After all, I've been in the system since I was 10 and am officially labeled a 'convict, 'so who would listen to what I have to say. Hell, I would even tell myself that most people would think that I had merely gone crazy. Nonetheless, I truly believe that I have to do something to try and save others from the nightmare that I am living.

One morning, I was woken up by a loud kick on my cell door. I jumped up, ready and alert for whatever was about to go down. I saw the trouble making guard that I had assaulted, standing on the other side of my cell door. Annoyed that it was *him* of all people who woke me, and not really being able to read his body language, I asked, "Whatta you want?"

Calmly he responded "I'm man enough if you're man enough."

I was still half asleep and totally baffled by what he had just said so I asked, "Man enough to what?"

Nonchalantly he replied, "To apologize." *Now that alone almost knocked me on my butt. The fact that a guard was apologizing to me was scarier than a beating.*

Fully awake now, but totally confused by his presence, I

said, "Okay, let me get this straight. You came all the way over here to solitary almost a year later for an apology?"

He answered, "Well, I've been assigned to this cell block now."

Nodding, I sarcastically respond, "great" and asked him if it really mattered if either one of us apologized after all this time. He told me that my boy, Elijah, had made parole a few days earlier and would be shipping out any day. Surprised I asked, "Is that right?" and he replied affirmatively. There was total silence. I told him that since we both knew that he was the one who brought the whole incident to a head, that he should apologize first. Instantly he said, "I apologize, and just so you know, I requested that the assault charge be dropped against you, but was informed that you would be transferred out as soon as your solitary time was completed."

Accepting his apology I said, "Alright. Fair enough. I too, apologize." After another short moment of silence he asked if I had been out of my cell much in the past year. Shaking my head I told him no, and he asked me if I would like to work for him by handing out the food trays in the cellblock. *By now I am TOTALLY flabbergasted, and start thinking that I was still asleep and that this whole scene was nothing but a dream.*

Now I'm really thinking that this guard must be up to something- he must have a plan to set me up. I then realized that he didn't have to go through this ordeal just to 'get me'. So I thought, 'What the hell.' If I agreed to work for this guard, I might be able to get to that so-called 'leader' of the anti-system faction who challenged me. The one who warned me that it was 'on the first chance we got.' I responded positively to his offer and told him that I'd work for him as long as he was on the 'up-and-up' about the whole thing. Then as if nothing ever happened between us, he unlocked my door and told me to follow him.

Eventually, the guard and I started talking. He told me that he took a look at my prison file. He cracked a smile and said, "Which by the way, took a long time since your file's the size of a suitcase." He continued the conversation by saying that by the time he had finished reading it all, he felt that I had been dealt a bad hand in life. He also told me that he didn't like convicts because they disgraced the human race, and that was the same view shared by everyone else within the organization that he belonged to.

So of course now I'm intrigued as to which organization he was a part of so I asked him, "Which organization do you belong to?"

Just as proud as he could be, he responded, "I'm part of the Klan *(Yes, that's right, the infamous Klan),* and our views aren't strictly based on race issues." I thought back to the day of the assault, and it dawned on me that Elijah is Puerto Rican, and I'm a cross-breed between Irish and American Indian. All that information is definitely in our records, and that's when I really got scared. I couldn't help but think to myself why a member of the Virginia Klan would apologize to me unless he was up to something. Up to my last day in solitary though, he never changed his demeanor towards me. As a matter of fact, he treated me as if he genuinely took a liking to me.

As soon as I came across the opportunity to meet up with the anti-system 'leader,' I did. While preparing to pass him his food tray through the cell door, we made eye contact and had I wanted, I could have run my arm through the bars and hurt him real bad. But while being face-to-face with him, I clearly saw the fear in his eyes that I was on the other side. I knew that the anti-system faction was the only thing that this guy had going for him, and the cause was

133

probably the only thing that got him from one day to the next within these walls of hell.

I realized that I was no one to be judging him for what his beliefs were, or for clinging onto others with similar beliefs. What he and his group believed in didn't affect me negatively in any way. After all, we are all living within the same nightmare together 24 hours a day, and I too have my own cause that gets me from one day to the next. Frankly, the thought of freedom and that long awaited date of release are the thoughts that I cling onto, and no one has the right to judge me for my cause or the way that I view things.

As we stared at each other I told him that I was KC, and then asked him if he wanted his food tray. Acknowledging who I was he simply said, "Good looking out KC, thanks a lot." Right then and there I knew that he wasn't your typical hardcore con, so I left it at 'live and let live'.

Chapter 14

Memphis, TN

A few days later, I was transferred out of Petersburg and into to the Federal Correctional Institution in Memphis. On the day of my transfer I had my last conversation with the guard who had befriended me. While on my way out to the bus, he told me to take care of myself and to give the guards in Memphis a break. Then he smiled and walked away.

Upon my arrival in Memphis, I was given the same old speech and sent right to solitary until I completed my *orientation period.* After I was released into general population, everything was actually going pretty smoothly. This all changed on the day that I decided to drink some home made wine with some of the established convicts. While drinking, one of the convicts offered me some pills. I swallowed the pills, and it was all down hill after that. I honestly can't remember a single thing that happened after I took those pills, but I was filled in later on.

Apparently, on my way back to my cellblock I approached a guard that was talking on the phone. With my shades still on, I casually walked up to him and tapped him on the shoulder. When he turned around to see who was there, I hit him right between the eyes. As he fell back against the wall, I simply kept on walking without ever saying a word to him, and went right into my cell where I passed out.

The next day I woke up in solitary, charged with another

assault on a guard. Since I couldn't even remember the incident, I thought that the guards had this whole thing planned out so that they could just keep me locked up. Oddly enough though, I couldn't even remember how I got to solitary, so I began to think that maybe I was guilty after all. Sure enough, it turned out that I had assaulted the guard who was talking on the phone. When I went before the judge, he sentenced me to another year in solitary, tacked an additional 5 years onto my sentence, and recommended that I be transferred to yet another federal prison.

While serving my time in solitary, I learned that no other federal prison wanted to take me in. The Director of Federal Prisons himself sent down an order from Washington, DC. His instructions were to confine me in what was called a 'box-car cell' all by myself, with absolutely no human contact. The box-car was a solitary cell with an adjoining cell that served as a buffer. Between the door of the buffer cell and my cell door, there was a table used by the guards where they could either push my food tray down with a stick, or slide it down into my cell. This way, the guards would never have any type of contact with me. I wasn't allowed any clothes, other than my shorts and socks. I wasn't allowed any type of property either.

One night, one of the convicts that worked in the plumbing shop came over to my box-car *(as if he were fixing something in one of the other cells)* and called out to me. He asked me if I was all right, and if I needed anything. I told him that the guards didn't allow me to smoke so I'd really appreciate some smokes and some matches. I told him to pass them off to the convict clerk that worked in the block so that he could slide them under my door. "You got it KC. Don't worry about it. I'll give them to the clerk on my way out because they searched me coming in, so I had to leave them upfront. Otherwise, I'd slide them to ya myself," he replied.

"No problem man, I understand. Thanks for looking out."

Several days had passed, and at this point, I was really looking forward to a smoke. The convict clerk still hadn't brought me the cigs though. I finally heard him outside my cell one day as he was sweeping, so I asked him if my boy had given him the smokes. *Now that was merely a rhetorical question because I knew that he wouldn't let me down.*

He replied, "Yeah- he gave them to me, but you're beat, dude."

I said, "Is that right?" Never once looking over at me, he had the nerve to tell me that since I was leaving soon, I didn't need the smokes. Trying to play the whole thing off so that he wouldn't know that I was mad as hell, I casually answered, "Maybe you're right." But in reality, all I was thinking about was how I was going to get that dude. I figured that the only opportunity I had to get to him was on shower day. Even though the guard would cuff me through the bars, I could push the cell door hard enough into him to hopefully knock him back. Then I could run out to where that dude sat, which happened to be right on the way to the showers. That's just what I did.

The very next day, I kicked the cell door into the guard so hard that it knocked him to the floor. I ran right to the convict clerk and began beating the crap outta him. When he finally fell, I started to slam his head into the floor. As he was calling out for help I said to him, "So you beat me outta my smokes, huh? Well beat this!" Tired of slamming his head into the floor, I got up and started to kick the crap outta him.

Finally, the guards got me off of him and knocked me to the floor. They beat and kicked me until I was nearly unconscious, and dragged me by my feet back into my cell. While lying on the floor, I

137

could see the guard who I hit with the door. I heard him tell another guard to call the Warden and ask him to come down because he thought that I had broken his nose when I kicked the cell door into his face.

He then turned towards me and I could see all the blood pouring down his nose on his face and shirt. Furious, he screamed, "Your days are numbered, animal! You're not only going to be charged with assaulting me this time, but also for assaulting my clerk!"

When the Warden arrived he asked how the clerk was doing, and instructed one of the guards to take him to the hospital for his head injuries. He then asked how I was, and the guard merely pointed towards me as I lay on the floor. After looking into my cell, the Warden instructed another guard to call the hospital and have them send someone over right away to look at me. Finally, he told the bloodied guard to go to the hospital himself and to give him a report in the morning.

As soon as the guard left, the Warden came back to my cell and asked me why I had assaulted the clerk. Since I didn't reply, he said, "Alright, you know what this means. You're getting another charge for assaulting a guard, and another one for assaulting an inmate,"

As soon as I got to the prison hospital, the nurse on duty took one look at me and said to the guards, "You've got to be kidding me! We can't take care of those injuries here- he's gonna have to go to the local hospital." They walked me out to the Administration Building and put me into one of the holding cells to wait until an ambulance showed up.

The pain was excruciating. I could see the bone sticking out of my right arm and it was very difficult to breathe while sitting, so I had to stand. The ambulance finally arrived, and the guards shackled my arms and legs before they loaded me in. When we arrived at the hospital the emergency room doctor told me that my arm had been broken in multiple places, and that I had three broken ribs. They gave me a local anesthetic, reset my arm, wrapped my ribs, and sent me back with the guards.

When we returned to the prison the Warden was waiting for me. He addressed the guards by telling them that from now on, under no circumstances should my cell be opened unless there were two guards present. He then addressed me by telling me that both the guard's, and convict's noses were broken and that I was in a heap of trouble. He also told me that he was going to make sure that time was added to my sentence for the assaults, which included an additional 3 years in solitary. He also told me that as soon as he could get me out of his institution, I was outta there.

About a month went by until one day, my outer door was opened by the Warden himself who was accompanied by two men wearing suits. One was standing right next to the Warden, and the other, although a bit out of site, appeared to be talking to the block guard. I heard the Warden say to the guy standing next to him, "That's Amos, the one we talked about. He's the one that no other institution was willing to take, so your Washington office instructed us some time ago to house him in the box-car until more permanent arrangements could be made."

Immediately after the Warden's introduction, the man walked into the buffer area between the cell doors, and walked towards me. With a somber face he said, "My name is John C. Smith, and I'm the Director of the Federal Bureau of Prisons. I must tell you, Mr. Amos, you sure have become the talk of my office, and I'm at my wits end because I don't know what to do with you." He continued, "Tell me

Mr. Amos, why are you so violent?"

I replied, "Well, Mr. Smith, being that this may be the only opportunity that I get to have a face-to-face with you, lets have a talk. Let me start by saying that I'm really not a violent person, but talking about violence Mr. Smith, take a good look at me. I have an arm with multiple breaks and three broken ribs. So if you'd like to talk about violent people, let's start with your guards. And I'm not just talking about the guards at *this* facility, but across the board. It's the prison *system* and your administration that force me to react in the manner that I do. As to what you're going to do with me, well sir, you have the power to release me- just let me go. That's all I want."

Seemingly amused by what I just said, both Mr. Smith and the Warden start laughing. I just shrugged my shoulders, turned around, and sat down. No sooner did my butt hit my bed than the other man wearing a suit came in and yelled, "Well, I'll be damned! Amos! What did you do now?"

As I look up, I see that it was the Klan guard who had befriended me while at Petersburg. *Apparently he was promoted into a big shot position in the Washington, D.C. office.* Grinning from ear-to-ear I replied, "You know, same deal, different day. Just trying to make it through another one." Mr. Smith then looked at the guard who was talking to me and asked him how we knew each other. With a half smile and a nod, the guard responded, "Amos assaulted me while he was in Petersburg. While he was in solitary I had the opportunity to get to know him. As a matter of fact, Amos, who's known as KC, turned out to be quite the convict and I even had him working for me. After getting to know him, I realized that KC is just like the rest of us, and is set in his own way. I honestly took a liking to him and after we made peace with each other, we never had a problem."

Mr. Smith looked at the Warden and said, "Well, we're having nothing but problems with him, isn't that right, Warden?" As the Warden nodded in agreement, Mr. Smith continued to say that in my short time here in Memphis, I had assaulted two guards and an inmate. He also said that I was so much trouble to the Bureau of Prisons that they couldn't get any other facility to take me. That's why I was in the box-car with a two guard hold at all times and absolutely no human contact.

"What is he asking for to resolve the issue?" The Klan guard questioned the men. Mr. Smith replied, "Hell, he just told me that I have the power to release him, and that I should grant him his freedom. He assured me that if I released him, the BOP would never see him or have to deal with him again."

As if given a cue, all three of them burst out laughing. When he was finally able to pull himself together, the guard who befriended me asked Mr. Smith if he had ever read my file. Winding down himself, Mr. Smith replied, "Yes, I've seen his file and he's a real thorn in my ass."

The same guard then reached over and put his hand on Mr. Smith's shoulder and said, "Boss, when you get a chance, take a real look at his file. Look back to when he first entered the *system* at 10 years old and you'll clearly see that we've lead him to where he is today." He then looked over to me and said, "KC, you can't be released until you've served your sentence, but is there a facility that you would like to be transferred to where life might be easier for you and the guards?" He then looked back to Mr. Smith and said, "I think he's been in the *system* for so long that he would do better in a traditional prison with older convicts." Mr. Smith looked over to me and asked how many years I had spent in solitary. Honestly I had lost count, but I knew it was somewhere in the area of 10 years total at this point. Taken back by my response, he yelled, "Damn boy! Haven't you learned anything yet?" Sarcastically I replied, "You mean- haven't your guards been able to destroy my mind yet."

With a smirk on his face he grumbled, "I see Amos. You know, I just opened a new prison in Oxford, Wisconsin. The Warden at Oxford is named Big John, and he's worked with cases like yours for years." He looked at the Warden and asked when I would be standing trial for the assaults. Quickly, the Warden told him within two weeks. Still addressing the Warden, Mr. Smith told him that once the assault issue was wrapped up, I should be given a try at Oxford. He told the Warden that he would give John a call to let him know that I would be coming for a little adjustment. As he turned towards me, Mr. Smith smugly smiled and asked how that sounded to me. He asked if I could give him my word that I'd stay out of trouble for at least 6 months.

Apathetically, I told Mr. Smith that I couldn't give him my word because unfortunately trouble always seemed to find me. Nodding his head he said, "Fair enough, Amos, but at least tell me that you'll give it a try."

Knowing that I had nothing to lose I shrugged my shoulders and replied, "Sure, Mr. Smith, I'll give it a try." As he walked out of the buffer area, I heard him tell the Warden to get me out of the box-car and into general population until I went to court, and to make sure that I was put on a bus to Oxford immediately after the trial.

Two weeks later I went to trial and surprisingly enough, one charge was dropped and the other was dismissed. The assault charge against the guard was dropped because of the extent of injuries I had received at the hands of the BOP, and the assault charge against the clerk was dismissed because he perjured himself during the trial. However, I didn't get off scot- free. I was sentenced to yet another year in solitary, and the very next morning I was put on a bus to Oxford, WI.

Chapter 15

Oxford, WI

Oxford was the largest prison I had ever seen thus far. It was built out in the middle of swamp country and was so remote, that even the guards had a difficult time getting there. Unlike other prisons, when we arrived at Oxford we didn't drive to the Administration Building. Instead we went into a sally port where a lot of guards were waiting for us. As soon as the bus parked, one of the Oxford guards boarded the bus and began role call. *There were 32 other prisoners on the bus with me.* He instructed us to respond 'here' when we heard our name and number, so that's exactly what I did when he called me. Unlike everyone else who responded, I was singled out and told to walk to the front of the bus, so I stood up and walked forward. When I reached the front of the bus, the guard doing role call told two other guards that were waiting outside that the Warden's orders were to take me straight to solitary. While walking to the solitary cells, I noticed that the guards used cars and golf carts to get around within the complex because it was so big.

As soon as I was processed into solitary and assigned to a cell, the other convicts started their grilling. One yelled, "Say dude! Where you coming from?"

Knowing the drill I answered, "Memphis Federal Prison". Another one asked, "Whatcha doing in solitary?"

Not wanting to publicize what had landed me there I merely said, "I was told that the Warden ordered me into solitary."

Someone else yelled, "That's not good, man. The Warden only greets trouble makers in solitary."

Then another convict chimed in saying, "Yo, man. Are you a trouble maker?" Apparently the Warden thinks you are, and that means that you're in some serious trouble already."

In an attempt to stop the line of questioning and comments I said, "Look man, I just got here. I don't know anything about being in trouble, but I can tell you all that I'm not looking for any. So just to let everyone know- my name is KC."

As soon as I stated my name, I could hear the guards coming down the hall and noticed that all the convicts became quiet immediately. I knew that something was going down and in the silence, I could hear foot-steps approaching my cell. A few seconds later, there was a man in a suit standing outside my cell door, accompanied by four guards.

Looking in at me, the man in the suit said, "My name is Warden John. I'm the one that Mr. Smith spoke with you about. I want you to know that you're here against my will, and that I was forced to take you in. I don't like you or anything about you, so let me make it perfectly clear that the first chance I get to send you elsewhere I will. I'll be looking for that chance. You also need to know that if you assault any of my guards or prisoners, you won't be going to trial like what you're accustomed to. I'll deal with you personally- Texas style."

I stood in my cell solemnly thinking to myself, 'What the hell is 'Texas style? Shit, this guy's huge, and his hands are three times bigger than mine, so it can't be a good thing.'

He then announced to all of the guards accompanying him, "If any of you have the slightest trouble with this convict, and I don't care how minor it is, you call me immediately so that I can get him

145

out of here. He has 2 years and 6 months to serve in solitary, and during that time he is to be on a two-man hold with absolutely no human contact until I say differently. All of his meals are to be served on paper trays, and he's only allowed to have socks and shorts- all other clothing is prohibited. The only property that he's allowed to have is a blanket and a sheet. We're in the process of having a single cage built outside for him, so until it's finished he's not to have any recreation. Once the solitary cell is finished, he's to be handcuffed during his entire hour of recreation. Do I make myself clear?"

On cue, all the guards eagerly responded, "Yes, sir"

He then said to me, "Maybe you'll change your ways while serving your time here, and by the way, welcome to Oxford." *Thinking back to that day, the whole thing seemed weird.*

Even though I was in solitary confinement with absolutely no human contact, my cell was searched twice a day. Following the Warden's lead, the guards tried for the longest to get a reaction out of me so that they could jump me and have me transferred out. No matter how sadistic they were, I wouldn't bite the bait. Before I knew it, I had only 6 months left to serve in solitary.

One morning, as he was making his rounds, the Warden stopped at my cell and asked how life was treating me. *Now all I'm thinking is- how the hell do you think it's treating me? I've been locked in solitary for over 2 years with nothing but a pair of socks, shorts, a blanket and a sheet, and then I'm shackled whenever I'm taken out to the pen you had built for me.*

So playing along I told him that even though life had given me a bad hand, I still tried to make it a winning hand one day at a time. He then asked me if I was from Texas. *I honestly didn't know why he asked me that question. He had my file and knew that I wasn't from Texas.*

When I told him no- I was from Kansas City, Missouri he replied, "Close enough," and continued, "Amos, during your entire time here I haven't heard any bad reports on you. What's the deal?" *By now I'm really lost in this entire conversation and can't figure out where he's going with all of this.*

When I asked him what he meant, he told me that I'd been locked down for over 2 years at Oxford, so how come I hadn't given any of his guards any problems. He then asked me if I was plotting something. *At this point I was truly convinced that he must have been on some kind of drug.*

As I smiled at him I said, "No, I'm not plotting anything. I just know that I can't win with the cards I'm holding. Besides, unlike many of the other guards in my past, your guards haven't given me any reason to give them any trouble."

Smiling back the Warden said, "Amos, if I were to release you early into population, do you think you could carry yourself in the manner you have so far?"

I coolly replied, "I'll sure try Warden. Believe me, it's not my will to be confined within a cage in a prison. But in case you're going to ask, I can't give you my word on this because as I've said in the past, trouble always seems to come my way."

Laughing out loud, the Warden said to me, "Alright Amos. I'm going to have you released and assigned to mail delivery duty. That means that you'll drive around the complex in a golf cart delivering mail to the housing units. Is that a job you think you can handle?"

Totally perplexed I replied, "Well, that sounds like a good hand Warden, but why the change of heart?"

He told me that he and Mr. Smith went way back, and for

147

whatever reason Mr. Smith seemed to have taken an interest in me, so Mr. Smith asked the Warden if he could work with me. He also said that I was a hard head, but then so was he. The Warden called over to the guard on duty, and instructed him to have me transferred into general population. That very afternoon I was released into 'gen pop' and started working.

Throughout my entire prison term, driving the golf cart around the prison complex was the best job I ever had. It took a while, but eventually the guards eased up on me a little bit, and when they did, I seized the opportunity to try and find a way out of Oxford. I found a couple of flaws in their security, but I needed the time and tools to make it work in my favor.

A year in general population passed and everyone seemed to know who I was. Some of the convicts had learned through other prisoners transferring in and out of Oxford that I had been incarcerated for a long time, and that I shouldn't be underestimated in any way. It seemed as if I was making it at Oxford without a whole lot of prison games. That is not to say that they weren't being played, but I wasn't being pulled into any of them, and that was a good thing for me.

But nonetheless, I wanted to make my move to freedom as soon as I got the chance. I needed to get in better shape, so I started using the free weights to work out every day since while in solitary I could only do crunches and push ups to stay fit.

Security was tight, but not nearly as tight as they thought since I had the ability to move around the complex somewhat freely. Even though the cost was high, I was finally able to get a bolt cutter that I could use to easily cut through the chain link fences. I found a blind spot in one corner of the double fence that wasn't visible to any of the guard towers. Apparently, the prison wasn't really worried about that particular corner since it was a prohibited area for convicts, but during my deliveries I could get into that area. No one would be able to see me, and if for some reason I was spotted, it would appear that I was just delivering mail to one of the shops.

During my reconnaissance missions, I noticed a spot under the first fence where the accumulation of water, combined with the digging of surrounding animals, had formed a natural hole. So to help it along, I poured a bucket of water into the hole, and then 'dug out' the softened dirt the next day. I would continue this process until the hole was big enough for me to slide underneath the first fence. I already had an extra blanket stashed away nearby that I could use to cover the barbed wire so that I wouldn't get cut up like I had back in El Reno. The plan was to use the bolt cutters to cut through the second fence, and run like hell into the woods. After digging for a week, the hole was just about big enough. One more good dig and I was home free!

Since the perimeter fences were inspected routinely, about every 3 weeks or so, I knew that I couldn't just leave it to chance that the guards would see the hole and fill it in. I had everything that I needed and everything was looking good. I decided that I was going to make my move the following week. While I was eating supper on the evening of my planned escape, one of the convicts that I knew who worked in the Processing Building, came in the mess hall and sat down with me. As soon as he sat down, he immediately told me that a dude just came through Processing who was transferred in from El Reno Federal Prison in Oklahoma. He had been asking everyone if there was someone called KC at Oxford. He said that it was pretty odd that as soon as the guy got off the bus he started asking questions like that, so he figured he'd give me a heads up and let me know. I immediately thanked him and asked what the dude's name was. He said that he really couldn't remember because they had processed a lot of guys that day, but that he overheard the Housing Guard assign him to our cellblock. He told me that as soon as we got back to our cells, he would point him out to me.

I told him okay, and thanked him again. While we finished supper, I kept thinking to myself, 'Who the hell from El Reno could be asking about me?' *Then for whatever reason Duke came to mind. He was the badass from El Reno whom I had shanked.* As soon as we were finished eating, we walked back to our cellblock and were locked in so the guards could do their count.

Once count was confirmed, we were allowed back out of our cage for an hour of recreation. The convict who tipped me off met me in the day room, and as soon as he saw the dude walked by, he nodded toward him. As I'm looking at the guy I said to the con next to me, "I don't know that dude, but you know what, guys are always acting like they know me or maybe trying to deliver a message from someone that I do know. I'm going to step out for a minute, but when I get back I'll make it a point to go talk to him. "Thanks again man. Good looking out."

I casually slipped out to the area where I had hid my shank, and as soon as I came back into the day room, I walked up behind the guy who had asked about me and said, "I'm KC. I hear you're trying to find out who I am."

Without turning around he said, "Yo, just like you I've been locked up for a long time, and I've heard a lot about you down the way. I was told by some of the guys I've served with that you might be in here, and that you're a good convict to know."

Skeptically I asked, "Who are you? If you've been in so long how come I've never seen you in any of the joints I've been in?"

Nervously, he said, "I'm Jimbo". *Now I'm thinking to myself-*

I don't know anyone named Jimbo. So I say, "Well, Jimbo, tell me who you're with *(meaning which clique do you run with.)"*

Oddly, he asks what I meant by that and I clarify by saying, "what clique are you with?"

He responded, "I'm on my own," and although I said "alright," I knew that was a lie. There's no such thing in prison- no one rides alone. Hoping to figure out what's on this guy's mind, I asked him where he was from. He tells me that he's outta St. Louis, Missouri. Right then and there I knew that he had to be one of Duke's boys, so I stepped back from him, acting like everything was cool between us. This way I could do some investigating of my own on this dude and find out why he's really trying to track me down.

By now it was too late for me to make my move out of Oxford, so I headed back to my cell. As I lay in my bunk, I kept thinking about this dude and what I may have to do. His presence alone was jeopardizing my escape plan. Eventually I dozed off, only to awoken by a real hard blow. As I tried to sit up, I noticed someone running out of my cell and immediately felt a sharp pain in my chest. When I looked down, I saw a shank sticking right out of my chest near my heart, and that my shirt was full of blood. Since I couldn't get up, I lay back down, grabbed the protruding end of the shank with both hands and quickly pulled it out of my chest. As I got up to walk toward my cell door, I also felt a pain in my gut. I had assumed that the chest wound had caused all of the blood on my shirt, but when I lifted my shirt away from my belly, I noticed that I had also been stabbed near my stomach. By the time I made it to my cell door, the guy who stabbed me was gone. I immediately realized that I had let my guard down, and that it was Jimbo who got me.

Although I knew I was in pretty bad shape *(blood was running out of my mouth with every breath, I was bleeding profusely through the gapping holes in my chest and belly, and the pain was excruciating),* all I could think of was evening the score. So with his shank in my hand I headed down the hall. Every step I took was more debilitating than the last, but I knew I had to keep going if I was going to catch up with Jimbo.

Despite my determination for revenge, I succumbed to my wounds and fell to the floor. As I lay there feeling as though I were dying, I kept telling myself to get up. This was a war zone and my enemy was watching. I couldn't go out this way.

Out of nowhere, my father's voice resonated in my mind as if he was standing right there next to me. An eerie feeling came over me as I heard him saying, "Son, the way you're headed if you're not dead by 21, you'll spend the rest of your life in prison." I felt as though I were bewitched by my father, and as I laid in a pool of my own blood I said to myself, 'So this is it old man, huh? Is this the way my journey in hell is suppose to end?' I then asked God, 'Are you finally going to speak to me now?' Not hearing a response I told myself, 'Man, as usual you're on your own here. You gotta get up!'

An old convict that I knew came running up to me and asked, "Who did this to you, KC?"

With barely the strength to respond I said, "I think it was that new dude, Jimbo, but I really don't know."

Crouching down next to me, almost shielding me completely with his body he said, "Don't worry, KC. I'm here now, and I won't let anyone get near you."

With barely the strength to talk I muttered, "Old timer, do me a favor and get rid of this shank for me."

He whispered back, "Alright KC, I got it." As soon as he removed the shank from my hand, I felt myself slip away.

When I finally woke up I noticed that I was in an offsite

hospital room, and that I had tubes running out of my body. I heard people crying, and still groggy from all the meds I thought to myself, 'what the hell's going on here?' Who are those people over there?' As I began to focus on my surroundings, I saw one tube coming out of my side that was full of blood, and that the people crying on the other side of the room were my mother and ex-wife. In a voice slightly louder than a whisper I asked, "Mom, why are you here, and why are you crying?" As they both walked over to my bed my mother said, "Danny, you were brought here three days ago and no one knew if you would wake up." Now in an uncontrollable sob, she hunched over the side of the bed. With one hand on my head, and the other holding my hand, she cried, "I'm sorry baby! I'm so sorry! Please forgive me for what I've done to you."

At that same moment, my ex-wife grabbed my other hand and squeezed it as if to let me know that she was also apologizing for her actions. I saw the door to my room open, and a priest walked in. He walked over to the doctor who was still standing on the other side of the room. Even with all the crying, I overheard the doctor tell the priest that I probably wouldn't make it through another night. I also heard the doctor say that my lung had been punctured, and that they couldn't stop the internal bleeding caused by the stab wounds to my belly.

Upon hearing that, I asked my mom and ex-wife if they thought I was dying. That was probably the worst thing I could have said because it caused them both to cry even more! I told both of them to stop crying because I wasn't going to die. Within a minute or so they eased up a little and eventually smiled at me. The doctor walked over to my bed and told my mom and ex-wife that he'd give them some time alone with me. As he looked my way and grinned, he walked out of the room.

153

While I was lying there, I thought to myself for a second that I must have paid off my worldly dues, and that the 'man upstairs' had forgiven me for whatever offences I had committed. I thought, 'Now what? My life can't possibly be over yet. Am I just imagining this whole thing? Have I finally gone crazy?'

After spending just a few minutes alone with the two of them, I told them to go home and get some rest because I was going to be fine, and they could come back and visit anytime. As my ex-wife walked out, she said, "KC, your daughter's name is Sydney Jolie, and she's beautiful.

Ironically, during my last escape 18 years ago, I tracked Sydney Jolie down (at that time she was about 30 years old and had children) because I wanted to find out once and for all if, in fact, she was my daughter. I asked her to take a blood test and although she agreed, she never showed up for the test. In the end I guess it wasn't important for her. After all, what difference would it make at this point in her life ... if I really was her father, I had missed everything anyway.

I was really feeling weird about the whole encounter, and as they left, the doctor walked back in and was accompanied by a guard. As the doctor started checking me over he said, "I don't believe this! I just can't believe this!"

Curiously the guard asked, "What?"

Then I said, "Doc, I don't want a guard to be the last thing I see before I die, so if that's what's happening, please tell the guard to leave my room."

Unexpectedly the doctor started smiling and said, "Son, you're not dying! You're gonna make it."

The guard couldn't keep quite so he said, "Huh? So how do you like that Amos? I guess that means that I'm going to be right

154

here watching ya," and then he smiled.

Totally confused by the whole thing, I asked the doctor why my mother and ex-wife were brought up from Missouri if I wasn't going to die? He told me that it was 'touch-n-go' for a while, but as it turned out, it was just a close call. He also said that he truthfully didn't understand how the situation turned itself around.

Still not understanding what happened, I asked, "Well, what close call are you talking about doc?"

He just shook his head, pressed his lips together and replied, "Some things are better off left alone and unsaid son."

Nodding in agreement I said, "Okay, doc, I understand what you're saying, but I want to be released and sent back to prison so I still have a shot at my delayed freedom."

The doctor put his hand on my leg and said, "Don't worry son. You'll only be here for a few more days." Sure enough, 3 days later I was sent back to Oxford.

As soon as I was admitted into the prison hospital, the Warden came to see me, along with the FBI. They didn't hesitate to ask who hit me. Of course, I told them that I didn't know since he snuck up on me while I was sleeping. The Warden then told me that he knew it was a waste of time asking, but it was something he had to do. He went on to say, "Just so you know, we have the convict that we believe did this to you locked up. Do you want to press charges? I mean for God's sake Amos! He almost killed you! We thought for sure that you were a goner because of the extent of your injuries, and just about took you off the count. If you don't help me here, I won't be able to put you back in general population and I'll have to transfer you to another prison."

Knowing that I wasn't going to testify against anybody I replied, "Look Warden, you still have the power to take me off the

155

count. Just release me and send me home." The Warden shook his head and told me that he really hoped that someday I got my freedom because I was a very interesting young man.

Chapter 16

Terre Haute, IN

Being that I didn't press charges against the convict that stabbed me, I was subsequently transferred to the United States Penitentiary in Terre Haute, Indiana. It was, and still remains to this day, one of the worst prisons in United States because of the extreme violence amongst convicts. The convicts in Terre Haute are hard-core cons who are 'jailhouse respect' extremists, and drug fanatics. It seemed that on a daily basis a convict would be killed over nothing. Inside Terra Haute, it didn't take much to start a war. A simple, 'Hey man! How ya doin'?' could you get you killed.

Although I had seen a lot of squirting blood from many severed throats, and had witnessed more stabbings than most forensic scientists will in an entire lifetime, I got sick to my stomach every time a hit went down. I actually saw a new arrival killed when he went to the mess hall to eat. He was looking around to see if there was anyone he knew so that he could bum a couple of smokes. Apparently, another convict noticed him looking toward his direction, so he walked up to him and asked, "Hey man, do you know me?" and when the new guy answered, "No, I don't think so," the other convict replied, "Then why the hell are you looking at me?" and shanked him to death right on the spot.

I couldn't figure out what was going on in there. It seemed like every convict's goal was to hurt or kill as many convicts as they possibly could! I frequently heard convicts bragging about how many more notches they had on their knife since they had entered Terre Haute, and how everyone's objective was being beat by the next guy's record.

Throughout the 5 years that I was there, that mentality never changed for the other convicts. All I could say was, "WOW ... this is crazy!" Fortunately, I didn't have any problems with any of the convicts or cliques at Terre Haute because I actually knew most of them from other prisons. I even met a guy named Hank who had also gotten into it with Duke, and wound up killing him. Ironically, the Administration determined that it was a 'self defense' situation, so Hank wasn't charged with Duke's murder. I even found out through the grapevine that Jimbo, the guy who hit me while I was in Oxford, was also killed. As it turned out, Duke put a contract out on me and hired some guys to make a move on me the first chance they got. Jimbo was one of those guys, but he wasn't in it just for the payout, he was just looking for a way to move up the ranks and boost his 'jailhouse respect'. When I think back to my time at Terre Haute, I still can't figure out the madness that takes place in there. The taking of so many lives was so senseless, yet a way of life for the survivors.

Chapter 17

Leavenworth, KS

After being in Terre Haute for 5 years, my case worker asked me out of the blue if I'd like a transfer to Leavenworth Penitentiary, which was in Kansas. *I was essentially being offered a ticket out of the psycho prison I was stuck in.* Without wasting a second, I quickly said, "Yes, Leavenworth would put me closer to home since it's only 28 miles from Kansas City."

"Well, the administration gave me a list of potential transferees and your name's on it, but I just wanna tell ya that you'll be the youngest convict to ever be sent there. Are you sure that you wanna be transferred there?" he queried.

Again I replied, "Yes."

"Okay, and just one more thing. Your father's no longer there. He's been moved out to the camps,"

Shrugging my shoulders I answered, "Where he is doesn't matter to me. I want to be transferred to Leavenworth to be closer to home, not him."

With a quick nod he agreed. "Alright, then. I'll approve you for the transfer."

Nodding in acknowledgement, I stood up and started to walk out of the room. Before I reached the door however, I casually asked how long it would be before I was shipped out. He informed me that it would be soon. Two weeks later I was told to pack up my things because I was being transferred to Leavenworth.

As the 'Con Air' plane landed at the Kansas City Airport, I saw the outline of the surrounding buildings through the window, and all that I could think about was that 'I'm finally home.' Just knowing that I was back home gave me a small, although false, sense of freedom. For a moment or two, I found myself back in society walking down the streets that I was kept away from for so long. *Even thinking about that today still brings about a feeling of relief.*

I was quickly brought back to the grim reality of my prison existence when the guard called out "Amos! Number 35782-115." *All I could think about now was, "Gees, why couldn't they just give me a little longer to savor my dream of freedom?"* I stood up with my hands chained and legs shackled, and walked down the stairs of the plane. Moving as slowly as I could, I soaked in the view of all the surrounding buildings. I knew that whatever lay ahead of me was worth it because I was able to have this moment, no matter how brief the walk in my hometown was. I felt my burning desire to be free intensifying with every step I took. I soon felt my right shoulder being poked as the guard walking behind me said, "Move it, Amos! Stop dragging your feet!"

By the time I boarded the bus there were quite a few convicts already shackled to their seats. We waited for a few more to be loaded, and then we were on our way. As soon as the bus started moving, the convict sitting next to me told me that he served a couple of bids (sentences) at Leavenworth, and that we were on our way to another world.

As the bus turned on to the long familiar roads which lead to the front of the large, white building and the big dome, I was instantly taken back in time to when I was 8 years old, accompanying my grandmother to visit my father. *I had flash backs of how once we reached the tower, the guard used a loud speaker to ask my grandmother to state her business. She would announce that we were there to visit my father. I also recalled the guard saying to me, "Son, you better be good for your grandmother and do what she tells you to do. Don't ever wind up here like your father, because if you come here, you're not going to like my house."*

As soon as the bus stopped the guards began to unload us. As I waited outside with the other cons, I saw that same large tower which housed a gun carrying guard that I remembered seeing as a child. I also saw the multitude of stairs that led up to the simple wrought iron gate, and remembered helping my grandmother up the 144 stairs that lead us past that gate, and into the dome where the visits were held. As I started walking up those very same stairs, this time as an adult with my hands and legs shackled, I began counting them out loud.

Curiously, the old convict walking next to me asked, "Why are you counting the stairs, KC?"

I told him that I wanted to see if there were still 144 stairs. Shocked by my response he asked, "What? How do you know that there are 144 steps? You've never been here before!"

Nonchalantly I replied "Yeah I have, and more than once."

Apparently still puzzled by how I knew how many stairs there were, he said, "You're not old enough to have been here before."

I looked at him and smiled, and knowing that I had him puzzled I said, "It's a long story." Seemingly still not believing me, he shook his head and replied, "KC, I think these people have gotten in your head and made you nuts.

Enjoying the moment, I simply laughed.

As soon as we reached the top, I looked over to the old convict and said, "Yup. There's still 144 stairs!"

161

Skeptically, he told me that I must be on dope because I was really out of it! Together we walked through the outer gates and past the same area that my grandmother and I had also gone through when we visited my father. *Being there brought back memories of the guard who searched us, and what he said to me as a boy. Still to this day, his words send a chill through my body.*

The voice of a guard shouting instructions brought me out of my past, and back into the present. He yelled out, "Listen up, convicts! This is what you are all going to do. You're going to walk through the prisoner's gate into the rotunda. When I call your name, you're going to stand there in place until everyone is called. Once everyone is accounted for, your chains will be removed and you will strip naked. You will then be taken to the Receiving Area where you will be sprayed for lice, and allowed to take a 3 minute shower. After being issued clothing, you will be assigned to a cellblock in the big house. If any of you have any questions, keep them to yourselves."

I couldn't help but laugh to myself. Some things never change. It's the same old routine where ever you go, and all of the guards are all the same- full of nothing but talk and always looking for a convict to hassle.

Fifteen minutes later, everyone was in the rotunda and once the chains were removed, we all started stripping down to our shorts. As I looked around, it hit me that the rotunda was actually the dome that I remembered as a child, and that the cellblocks ran off of the dome. I then noticed a bunch of convicts standing at each of the huge barred doors that led to each cellblock, and a few seconds later, the obscenities started flying. The convicts at the doors started yelling, "Say baby, I want you in my cell tonight; I wanna kiss you all over your body; Man, we're going to get married; I've been waiting for you to come to me for years."

162

If that wasn't degrading enough, the guards joined in by saying, "I told you cons to strip naked! You can all go meet your husbands once I'm through with you. Don't worry, you'll have plenty of time to get acquainted because no one comes to Leavenworth for a short stay. Welcome to a world of it's own. While here, some of you will die of natural causes, some will have your right to live taken away by your husband, and some will die trying to take on a wife. Bottom line is, as soon as we get this process done and over with, the sooner you can all start your new lives!"

This was definitely unfamiliar territory to me. After hearing all those catcalls and the guards announcement, I thought to myself, 'what the hell was that all about'? That's the sickest thing I've ever heard.' At that very moment, I feared for my life. I knew right from the start that there were hard times ahead, and that there was no chance of escape because of the 45-foot walls that surrounded the place. Not only were the walls unscaleable, but they were so thick that they served as an 'internal' road. The guards literally drove on the wall to set up lookouts wherever they thought a problem might erupt in the prison yard. I told myself right there that I'd have to keep moving forward and just deal with whatever came my way.

While I was in line in the Receiving and Discharge area waiting to use the shower, I saw a couple of long tables with cons working behind them. They were handing out clothes and property. I also noticed that everyone who came in on the bus with me had a box with their name on it waiting behind the tables. The boxes contained their property, as well as stated what prison they were coming from, and where their final destination was, since not everyone would be staying at Leavenworth.

Early on I was told that in the Federal system, it wasn't uncommon for prisoners to be held for a few weeks, or even a few

163

months at a time in an interim prison. As a matter of fact, on a daily basis the Federal system typically shuffles about 2,000 convicts either in the air, or traveling on the ground between facilities. That intentional shuffling is often referred to as "air therapy, and is commonly used by the system to keep gang bangers, trouble makers, or 'enemies of the system' virtually untraceable. Convicts would essentially be kept on the move so as not to stay anywhere long enough to receive their property, make a phone call, or send and receive mail. They would have to spend most of their time in solitary awaiting their next transfer.

After we were done showering, we went over to the tables and stood in line to pick up our clothes and property. When it was my turn, the convict working behind the table only handed me my clothes, so I asked, "Hey, man. What's up with my property box?"

He looked at me and said, "You're not staying here."

I became angry at his response, and yelled, "Yes, I am! I was transferred here. This isn't a lay over for me, man! Just give me my stuff!"

Still not understanding, he said, "How old are you? As a matter of fact, don't bother answering. I know you're too young to be doing time in Leavenworth so there must be a mistake here." He called over one of the guards and said, "Hey, boss, I think there's a mistake here. This kid's box is labeled Leavenworth."

The guard looked at me and uttered, "Yeah, this must be a mistake. You're too young for Leavenworth." He walked over to the guard handling the actual paperwork and asked to see my transfer papers. As he was walking back towards us and reading my papers, I heard him say, "He is assigned to Leavenworth!"

In retrospect, since neither the guard nor the convict knew my history, they must have thought that I looked very young-

probably not much different than a school kid.

"Let me get on the phone with Captain Boyd to find out how they made this mistake." The distance between the phone and where I was standing was about 3 feet, so I could hear the guard saying, "What? You mean to tell me that this kid is staying here?" After about a minute of silence he said, "Have you taken a look at his mug shot? He looks like a school kid! Captain, there's no way that we can put this kid into general population. He won't last a day- they'll rape him or kill him!" After about another minute or so he said, "Okay, I'll see you at Receiving," and he hung up the phone.

The guard looked at the convict who was working the table, and then at me. "In the 20 years that I've been here, I've never seen a convict as young as you get sent to Leavenworth. You're by far the youngest convict to ever come through here. What did you do to be sent here? How many people did you kill to get a life sentence at such a young age?"

Not knowing exactly how to react to his seeming concern, I answered, "Look. I don't know why you would care anyway. Where were you years ago when I was a lot younger and was being tossed into the worst prisons?" Hearing no response from him to my question I continued, "I agreed to come to Leavenworth because I'm from Kansas City, and I expect to be placed into general population like all the rest of the cons. I'm not concerned about the age difference or the level of prison violence, and I'm sure not looking for any special treatment. This place can't possibly be any worse than where I just came from."

A bit irritated by my bluntness the guard said, "I won't be responsible for releasing you into general population. They'll eat you up alive in here, son. I don't care how dangerous you think it was where you just came from."

165

Then the old convict that I had travelled with said, "Man, wait until the other cons hear about you!" Unsure of how to take his comment I queried, "What are you saying?"

With a smile on his face he replied, "Oh, no disrespect intended. I just meant that you'll be like a baby here in Leavenworth. Hell, the cons will welcome you like anyone else. It's just that we've never seen this before, and I've been in and outta Leavenworth for 20 years. Honestly, I doubt that Captain Boyd will approve your being released into general population. He'll probably just have you transferred out." Then he said, "I see 'KC' tattooed on your neck. Is that your name?"

"Yes," I answered.

"Man, you have a lot of home-boys here. I'll make sure to let them know about you just in case they lock you up. That way they can get you some smokes and a few other things you'll need- if that's alright with you of course."

"Sure. Thanks for looking out. If they do lock me up, tell my home-boys to talk to the Administration to get me released into general population. Tell them that my father, Wade Amos, was just transferred to the camps from here."

With a surprised look the convict said, "I know Wade. You're his son?"

As I nodded I said, "Yeah."

Everyone knows your dad, even that guard that was questioning whether you should be here or not knows your dad. As a matter of fact, Wade used to work down here."

The old convict called the guard over and said, "Boss, guess whose son this is?"

"Whose?" The guard asked.

"Wade Amos," the convict informed him.

Clearly shocked, the guard replied, "No way" and looked at me asking, "Is that right, kid?"

"Yes," I answered indifferently.

The guard said, "Hell, you just missed him son! He went out to the camps just a couple of weeks ago."

"Yeah, I know," I replied, and left it at that.

Finally, Captain Boyd (a real big dude) arrived and asked the guard, "So where is this guy?" The guard looked over at me and with a nod, told me to come over. As soon as Captain Boyd saw me walking towards them he yelled, "Oh hell, no! Boy, you're not going into my general population! What the hell was the BOP thinking? There must be a mistake with the paperwork. I've gotta call Washington, DC! The only problem is what the hell am I going to do with you until I can get you transferred outta here?"

Almost stepping on his words, the guard said, "Cap. Guess who his father is?"

With a puzzled look the Captain asked, "Who?"

Eagerly the guard replied, "Wade Amos, the old convict that worked for me and was recently transferred out to the camps."

Intrigued by what he had just heard, the Captain said, "Is that right?"

After the two of them had finished their conversation about how I was nothing more than a school boy, I said, "Captain Boyd, I want you to know that my transfer to Leavenworth is not a mistake and that it was sanctioned by the BOP. Obviously, you haven't read my file, otherwise you'd know that I'm not the school boy you think I am and as a matter of fact, I've been locked up since I was 10. I know how to do my time."

As if I were just talking to myself he looked at the guard and snickered, "Did you just hear what that little brat said?" Looking

167

back at me he arrogantly said, "Look kid, although I couldn't care less about how long you've been locked up, bottom line is, you're too young to be here. If I were to release you into general population with these animals, I couldn't sleep right. If they don't kill you, you'll become one of their wives, and that's something that I'm not going to have over my head. So, you're going into solitary until I can ship you outta my prison."

Furiously I replied, "Well, listen! I couldn't care less about your sleep, what's over your head, or what you think. I'm not kidding with you- my transfer to Leavenworth was approved, and I expect to be treated just like every other con that is serving time in the Federal System. I'm not worried about all that crap you're trying to scare me with, so save it for the next guy."

Totally dismissing what I just told him, the Captain said to the guard, "Take the brat to solitary."

I was in solitary for 6 months until one morning a guard came to my cell and said, "Captain Boyd wants to speak with you, so put your clothes on and come with me."

The guard escorted me to Captain Boyd's office and when I went inside, the Captain said, "Sit down, Amos. Before I say anything else I want you to know that I've called you in here against my will. Although I run this prison, I don't run the BOP in D.C., and if my boss tells me to do something, I have to do it. I've been ordered to release you into general population even though I doubt that you're going to last a day. But who knows? Maybe you'll make it in here, and if for some miracle you do, don't expect to be treated any different than any other convict here- understood?"

Knowing I was finally getting outta solitary I said, "Captain, I wouldn't have it any other way."

Acknowledging my acceptance of his statement he nodded

his head and said, "Okay then. You'll be temporarily assigned to Building 63. It's an older building that divides the receiving block, and solitary confinement. There's a lot of history in that building, actually there's a lot of history here in Leavenworth. You'll learn all about it while you're here. Anyway, you'll be housed in Building 63 for 2 weeks, and then you'll be transferred out to cellblock A. It holds 600 men and is a city within a cellblock. A-block is the most dangerous unit at Leavenworth; you name it and you'll find it in A-block. Unfortunately for you, all new arrivals go there first. Any questions?"

"No."

"Well, you know how things get around in the joint. I heard that your home boys from Kansas City have been asking for you to be released into general population and that they have your back. For once I hope that's true, because believe me, you're gonna need them. Anyhow, I know it's a waste of time, but I'd like to offer you protective custody until I can get you transferred elsewhere."

With a smirk I replied, "No thanks, Cap, that's not my style and besides, I've spent enough time locked up in solitary as is!"

With a smile he said, "Alright. Consider yourself released into general population. The property room will call you to pick up your belongings when they're ready for you. For now, just report to 63-block for a cell assignment. Go down the hall all the way to the end, and go through the doors to the yard. The first building on your right is number 63. When you go inside, ask for the guard and he'll assign you your housing. Know that you're on your own now... I hope to see ya around."

As I stood up I said, "Alright, Cap," and I walked out.

The minute I left the Captain's office I noticed a whole bunch of older convicts standing in the hall. As soon as a couple of them saw me approaching they tapped each other on the shoulder and one yelled out, "Hey, young Kansas City! Hold up!"

I stopped and asked, "What's up?"

As a few of them walked up to me, one of them said, "I'm Ben, and we're a few of your home-boys. We hear you're from KC."

I replied, "Yeah, I am. My name's KC."

Then the one doing the talking said to the others, "Aint that something! He just got here and he's already taking over the big house."

Smiling, I said, "'No, it's not like that. I earned my name." They all busted out laughing. Laughing along with them I asked, "What's so funny?"

One of them said, "Hell, son. We thought all the gangsters were already locked up in Leavenworth!"

Nodding, I replied, "Well, I have to get over to Building 63."

Someone then said, "No problem. We already set everything up for you over there. Anything that we thought you might need is waiting for you in your cell. You've been assigned to the cell that the Birdman from Alcatraz had while he did his time here."

Unfamiliar with whose cell I would be taking, I asked, "Who was he, a homeboy?"

One of them said, "No, just a crazy convict who loved birds and kept them in his cell."

Fascinated by what I was told I said, "Is that right? Or are you guys just putting me on?"

Almost on cue they all became straight faced and said, "No. He really was here, and now you're assigned to his cell. Of course he's long gone. He died years ago, but he served 26 years here before being transferred to Alcatraz. Look KC, all of the home-boys are going to be out in the yard waiting for ya. So as soon as you get yourself together, come on out. A lot of the old timers want to meet you- they're not going to believe how young the BOP is shipping folks down to Leavenworth. Besides, there are a lot of your old man's friends out there."

Gratefully I said, "Alright, but let me express something to you all so that you can let the other home-boys and every one else know. I'm not gonna be anyone's kid. I'm not looking to start trouble with anyone, and I'm sure not gonna take it from anyone. If there's anyone out there that is planning on killing me, then let's get it over with. Just be fair about it and give me a shank so I can at least have a chance."

They immediately started laughing as if I had just delivered the punch line to a belly-aching joke.

Insulted by their laughter I told them, "Look, I don't find this funny, and I don't expect you to treat me any different than you would any of the other convicts. I know how to do my time."

Obviously seeing how serious I was about the whole thing, they backed off and one of them said, "First of all, we put a shank inside your sheets for protection. No one in Leavenworth, including us, has a beef with you. You're our youngest home-boy and everyone is going to be happy just having you around. Hell, maybe your young spirit will rub off on some of us old timers!"

One of the other convicts agreed by saying, "I sure do hope so, KC!"

The conversation took on a more realistic tone when another con said, "Now as for you being treated no different than anyone else here, we don't care how many wars you've survived, or how many victims you may have under your belt. You need to know that some of the cons here came from Alcatraz and Marion, (the joint that replaced Alcatraz) and that most of us old timers have been here for

171

a long time and are never getting out. We don't know where you stand as far as ever wanting to get out or not, but it doesn't matter one way or another. This is the big house, and next to Marion and Alcatraz, there is no worse place to be. So like it or not, you will be treated differently because there are a lot of crazy convicts here with a head full of bad wiring, and in this place we all need someone watching our back. The deal is that we knew about you as soon as you got here. The Captain called us into his office and gave some of us the low down on you. He told us that the BOP had finally gone mad and sent a kid to Leavenworth. He said it was a kid who had a prison record filled with so much violence that it made some of our records look squeaky clean. He told us that with your temperament you would fit right in with some of these thugs and that you wouldn't last a day in general population, but that he was forced to release you from solitary. So like it or not, we look out for each other here-young and old alike. Since you're the youngest to ever do a bid in Leavenworth, you are the baby. Of course there's no disrespect meant by that label, but until you're aware of everything going on in this prison and get to know who's who, you will be treated with respect. If anyone hurts you in any way, there will be repercussions and unfortunately you have no say in that. However, we want you to be yourself and continue carrying yourself in the manner in which you have been since you started serving time. Don't feel awkward when offered items from the old cons we introduce you to. They have children your age and would be offended if you didn't take their gift. We don't care whether you want them or not. You can do whatever you want with them later on, but right now don't disrespect or dishonor them and take whatever they give you. KC, we're not trying to belittle you in any way. We just want you to know that we are on your side and that neither guard nor convict will mess with you. Your father had a lot of respect in here and that carries over to you. Got it?"

Well after that lecture what else could I say but, "Got it."

Finally someone said, "Okay, then. We'll see you on the yard." As one of them opened the door for me, I walked out and headed to Building 63.

As I walked away from them, I felt like a piece of meat being thrown to the wolves. On the other hand, I felt a sense of belonging come over me. Although that was a good feeling and one that I hadn't experienced in a very long, long time, I knew that I still had to be cautious.

As I entered Building 63, the guard on duty asked, "Are you KC?" When I responded affirmatively, he said, "You've been assigned to the 'Birdman's old cell. It's the double cell in the far back. The pipes running across the room are where his birds would perch, that's the only reason they're exposed. You're the only one assigned to that cell, and if it hadn't have been for your home boys filling it up with all kinds of stuff, you would have had a lot of room." *I now knew that the old timers weren't in fact BS-ing me.* He then said something that almost knocked me on my butt. He said, "Anyway, if you have any candy bars in there, how about letting me have one? They call me the 'Candy Man' around here."

Looking at him in shock because he must have weighed at least 300 pounds, I nodded and said, "Sure. Let me go see what I have." I could barely believe my eyes when I entered my cell. It was stock full of everything that anyone would need in prison! I had all kinds of canteen items and when I checked for candy bars, there was a sack full of them! As I looked around the cell I saw the pipes that the guard was talking about where the Birdman's birds had perched. I also saw another door, which was closed off, near the back of the

173

cell that led to a small, enclosed yard where I presume the Birdman spent his rec time. The guard, known as the Candy Man, came in and asked, "So, do you have any candy bars?"

"Yeah, here you go." He thanked me and walked away. I actually thought he was pretty-funny, and God knows that no other guard ever came across to me like that before! I decided to leave everything as it was and unpack later. I wanted to go out into the yard and find out where these dudes were coming from. As I passed my bunk however, I checked the sheets and found the shank that the old timer said was hidden there. I grabbed it, put it in my pocket, and walked out into the yard.

As I entered the yard, I quickly saw my home-boys. There seemed to be a whole lot more of them than I expected. As I walked towards them, I noticed they were all looking at me and talking amongst each other. I couldn't hear what they were saying, which made me feel uneasy. I just told myself, 'KC, you're going to get through this. Just keep walking. You're stuck in this *mad house* just like they are.

As I moved forward, I scoped out the surrounding walls. Right from the start I didn't see any way of getting out of Leavenworth. The walls were huge and there were gun towers at every corner, and even in-between; something that I never saw as a visitor! Being so close now, I could see that they didn't use rifles or shotguns, but had machine guns at every post! The site triggered a flashback to someone I met years ago. His name was Otto and like me, he was all about trying to escape. He once told me that he tried going over a wall at Leavenworth with his partner but they didn't make it. Well, now being in Leavenworth, I see why.

As I continued toward my newfound home-boys, I noticed a huge, ugly, green building off to the side and wondered what it was

174

used for. I later found out that it was referred to as the 'Green Monster', and was the P.I. (Prison Industries) Building. There they manufactured army uniforms, prison clothes, boots, etc. You name it and they made it! Eventually I learned that prisons (in addition to making money off of the convicts for the *system's* use) also used the convicts to manufacture goods for public and private businesses. Essentially, convicts were no more than slave laborers. We got paid 20 cents an hour while the prison system was making a mint on us. P.I.'s exist all over the United States. Within the Federal System the P.I.'s are known as "Unicore," and in the state of New Jersey specifically, the P.I. is known as "Deptcor." Believe it or not, they proudly advertise on their website that "Deptcor is an entity within the New Jersey Department of Corrections" and that they "manufacture products and render services from 23 shops within the state and county correctional facilities." They even post a mission statement - "Our purpose is to provide inmates with viable real-world work opportunities which can lead to meaningful employment upon release, and to provide quality manufactured goods/services to government agencies and public schools with the goal of saving taxpayer dollars."

What a lie! In other words, they legally exploit their prisoners for a profit! *While I was imprisoned in New Jersey, I earned less than $10.00 a month. Where are the Labor Board and the Human Rights Activists now?*

I could never understand why every year the State and Federal Government collected taxes from the public in order to house prisoners. Since they pay us 'slave wages', how could they claim that the money they're collecting per convict' isn't enough? Maybe if they used some of that money to implement viable programs that would actually prepare convicts to succeed in the 'real world', then perhaps I could understand their dissatisfaction with how much they're collecting. The way I see it, as long as the Administration, and everyone under it continues to milk the system for every dime, prison will continue to be a lucrative business for the government. I mean, there's gotta be a reason why America 'warehouses' more people than any other country!

According to a 2004 study, the United States has the largest documented prison population in the world with about 2,135,901 people behind bars. That equates to approximately 724 people out of every 100,000. The report also indicated that if you include all 5,069 penal facilities across the country, the capacity of the 'official' prison system is only 1,951,650 people. You do the math.

As I moved closer to my home-boys, I saw that they were just laughing and joking around. Most of them seemed drunk, so I guessed that they were drinking some home made wine. When I walked up to the group I said, "What's up home-boys?"

Someone replied, "'It couldn't be better, son."

I think those words brought the biggest smile that my face could handle because I knew that they were having a grand ol' time.

As another con from the group offered me a jar full of wine, another one yelled, "Hey! Wait a minute! Don't you know that it's illegal to give under aged kids wine? You know you can go to jail for that!"

We all broke out laughing as they handed me the jar. I sat down and started drinking, and one of the older cons said, "See, that's what I'm talking about. If he's old enough to do time in Leavenworth, then hell, he must be old enough to drink!" The laughter just intensified after that and I instantly knew that the older cons were getting a kick outta me being so young and in Leavenworth.

Most of the cons greeted me with a hand shake and a couple just said, "How ya doin' KC?"

I replied, "Not bad. I'm glad to meet ya!"

One of them remarked, "Hell! That's the first time in years that I've heard anyone say that they actually were glad to meet me!" The same man then said, "Yo, KC, you may have to eat those words down the road son, because I hate everyone in the world!" He started laughing again.

When everyone finally piped down enough so a conversation could be held without having to yell over each other, one of the cons said, "Say KC, what's this we hear about your old man knowing you were coming to Leavenworth, so he begged the Warden to send him to the camps so that he wouldn't have to see you? Were you so damn mean as a kid that he robbed banks so he could come to Leavenworth to get away from you too?"

At that point the wine was starting to kick in so I was feeling a bit 'happy-go-lucky'. Without much thought I just said, "Alright! The jokes on me!" Then someone asked me what I thought about the big house so far and I replied, "Prison is prison to me, and I don't like any prison!"

They all nodded their heads in agreement. "Now that's a man who doesn't mind expressing how he feels or where he stands," one of them stated.

Then Ben, the first home-boy I met, said, "Hell, you all haven't heard nothing! He flat out told me that he wasn't going to be anyone's *kid*, or take any BS from anyone here, and that I should pass that along to all you thugs! Right then and there I knew this kid was a slice right off the block, so I told him the deal. I told him that no disrespect was intended, and that we have his back."

Another con put his two cents in and said, "See Ben over

here, he already warned all of us that no one's messing with your backside, but here he is telling you that we all got your back!"

After a minute of laughing the same con said, "All kidding aside KC, watch out for Ben. He's a dirty old man!" and the laughing kicked right back up.

A few minutes later the oldest looking con *(he must have been over 60 years old)* said, "Well, fellas, I think KC has definitely made his point and if any one of you thugs tries to mess with his back side, you'll have to go through me." He then extended his hand and said, "My name's Mario. I own a lot of clubs in Kansas City. Obviously we're all messing with you son, and of course we mean no harm. We're just having a little fun with you, but this is my prison and as long as I'm still kicking, you'll have me standing back-to-back with ya. I've been in and outta this place for a long time, and I still have a long ways to go. Actually, you don't remember me, but I remember you. You were the one always trying to hustle up some money by shining shoes at Big Bear's place downtown. As a matter of fact, you shined my shoes quite a few times so as far as I see it, you and me are all right. The only way you could piss me off is if you ever said that my cooking was bad! So as long as you don't cross that line we're straight- deal?"

Smiling from ear-to-ear I said, "You got it, Mario!"

Mario always made sure that I had at least three of his meals every week, and would regularly send for me to come down to his ten-man cell where I would gamble with him and his friends on the weekends.

I found that life in Leavenworth moved forward for me, and like the guard said upon arrival, "A- Block was a city within a cellblock." I also discovered that depending on where you went inside the cellblock, it could be an extremely violent place. I noticed that the majority of the cons there had tattoos and I decided to get a few too, so I went down to the corner tattoo shop- so to speak. As it turned out I actually knew the convict that ran the tattoo shop from another prison. After talking to him he gave me a few binders to look through and told me to pick out the pattern I wanted. He told me that he charged according to how much work I wanted done, and not necessarily per pattern.

Before I knew it, I was covered with tattoos. I never worried about the guards asking any questions since they also shopped at the tattoo parlor in A-Block. You could also 'buy' yourself an education in A-Block and become whatever you wanted.

For a small fee, you could receive a certificate that could be extremely helpful when going before the parole board. They would get all hyped up on convicts obtaining an education while incarcerated. Being that I could barely spell my name and probably had the I.Q. of 19 boxes of rocks, I knew that I needed to buy a G.E.D. I went to see the con that ran the print shop and told him what I was looking for. He told me that a G.E.D. was a 'run of the mill' certificate and that he could get me one in a couple of days in exchange for a carton of smokes. I told him that was no problem, and that I would be able to pay him during rec time. As promised, a couple of days later as I was coming out of the mess hall, he caught up to me and said, "Hey KC. I finished the work you wanted and I could bring it by your cell tonight after count if that's okay."

"Sure, that's perfect. Thanks."

Over a year went by and I remained in A-Block which as it turned out, was indeed everything it was cracked up to be. There wasn't anything you couldn't get. There were wine dealers who charged five dollars for a quart of wine; prison tailors who made custom clothing; shoemakers who could make a custom pair of shoes with the best leather available from the 'Green Monster' stock, and there was every kind of drug imaginable. As a matter of fact, there was more dope being dealt in that cellblock than anyone could ever imagine. During my time there I made my rounds to every 'store' on the block, and I felt like a million bucks! For the first time in my life I truly felt that I could live as well as any other con, and that things were finally looking up for me. However, the violence was extremely brutal. Within my first year in A-Block, there were at least ten murders and countless assaults that resulted in severe wounds. It was a killing zone and I had to stay alert at all times. It was impossible to know what, or who was waiting around the next comer.

Until I went to Leavenworth, I thought I had seen it all. I believed that I had lived within the worst prisons, but I soon discovered that was not true. In Leavenworth, the sex abuse was rampant and convicts even prostituted themselves for cigs. Some even dressed like women. Hell, I think some of them thought they really were women!

You could be killed for any reason in Leavenworth. If you unintentionally witnessed something going on in a cell, you had troubles. Convicts that accidentally saw someone with considerable 'jailhouse respect' engaged in a sexual act were usually killed. The things that I saw in there were so sick that I learned early on to keep my eyes looking forward and avoid, at all cost, looking into any of the cells as I traveled through the block.

Sometimes unavoidable situations presented themselves and I didn't have any control over them. I was specifically warned about this one convict named Scorpion *(apparently he earned that name because he killed every con that he had a sexual encounter with)* who was housed on the fifth floor. I was told to always keep my eyes open when going up there because he usually scoped out who he wanted, and waited for them to go up to the fifth floor. Once on his floor, he'd catch you off guard and rape you at knife point.

One day I unfortunately had to run up to the fifth floor. From the moment I set foot on that tier, I kept hoping that I wouldn't run into this guy. All I wanted to do was run up, take care of my business, and get back downstairs as quickly as I could. I didn't even make it half way down the tier when Scorpion jumped right out in front of me. He was covered in blood and holding a shank. He stared me dead in the face for about 30 seconds before turning around and running down the tier towards the area that I was headed. Needless to say, I didn't take care of any business on that floor that day. I just high-tailed my butt back downstairs. As soon as I could, I pulled one of my home-boys aside and told him what had happened. Incredibly, he just laughed. He eventually saw the alarmed look on my face and as he put his arm around my shoulders, he reassuringly said, "Listen. There was word on the line this morning that he was going to kill his cellmate today. You must have just run into him as he was leaving the area where he killed him." About an hour later we all watched as the guards hauled Scorpion away in cuffs. I later found out that's exactly what happened.

After 3 years in Leavenworth, I started using heroin. Not surprisingly, I got strung out on the stuff and had to start selling dope in order to make money to support my habit. You could literally sell dope all day in Leavenworth and never run out of product. Usually, the dealers would front you a gram of heroin, which was enough for ten decks. *A deck was basically a 10th of a gram packaged in either waxed paper or aluminum foil.* Each deck would cost $10 and you'd have to sell eight- the other two decks were yours.

This went on for over a year, but it eventually got so bad that

I had no choice but to go cold turkey. I couldn't sell enough to maintain my habit, and I became so sick from withdrawals that I wanted to die. The pain was agonizing and I became totally debilitated.

Fortunately, my home-boys helped me through the ordeal by bringing me food and staying with me. Since kicking the habit and getting past that nightmare, I've never touched the stuff again. As soon as I was strong enough, I started regaining my health and working out with weights. One day while working out in the yard, some Hispanic dude came up on me and told me that I was short on the amount of money that I owed one of the dealers I used to work for. He told me that the dealer wanted the remainder of his money, or that I would have to work it off by selling dope for him again.

Knowing that this was a load of crap, I said, "We both know that there's no money owed to any of you. I never beat you, or anyone else for that matter, out of a cent. Look, I don't want anything to do with that stuff anymore so go back and tell your people that I don't owe them anything. They're not getting any money from me and I'm not gonna deal for them either."

I didn't find out until sometime later that the dealers I worked for were part of a major Mexican clique that dominated the drug trade in Leavenworth. Rumor had it that someone had beaten them out of some money, and since I hadn't been around for a while due to my withdrawals, they automatically thought it was me.

Since I just kept on working out, the messenger eventually walked away. Another Hispanic gang member went to my home-boys and ran the whole thing down to them. As soon as I got back, my home-boys told me that there was a big mess with the Hispanic crew because they said that I shorted them out of some money, and they expect to get it back.

Immediately shaking my head I said, "That's not true. If they're short, it wasn't me who shorted them. I'm not going to feed into their game."

Another one of the home-boys then said, "Well, we may have to go to war with the Hispanics."

"No. Let me handle this. I know the leader, and I did him a favor years back so he owes me. I'll put an end to this whole thing tomorrow morning. There's no way we are going to war over some lie!"

Coincidentally, the Hispanic crew's leader, Tito Colon, and I worked together in the prison laundry, so as soon as I saw him in the morning I said, "Tito, I need to kick it with you."

"About what. KC?" he asked

"Look man, you and I go way back and you know that I've always been a standup guy. I've never beat anyone outta anything."

He coolly shrugged his right shoulder and simply said, "Okay."

In spite of everything that had happened with his home-boys, I just wanted to make sure that we were both on the same page, so I said, "Well, your people are passing down messages that I beat them outta some dope money, and there's even talk about going to war over the whole thing."

Calmly he replied, "KC, I heard about it this morning. I realize that you take care of your business, and that you wouldn't lie about some chump change. Trust me, I'm not worried about it because I know that you weren't the one who beat us. Sorry to say, but I've got a lot of knuckleheads around me, and they sometimes shoot their mouth off too much. Now about the war- there won't be one, and whoever said that there would be, will now have to deal with me. You go tell your home-boys that I'm taking care of this. As for us, it's all good. You downed a guard for my sister's kid, Elijah, years back and I owe you one for that."

I quickly cut him off. "Nah, Tito. You don't owe me anything. What I did back then was the right thing to do. Elijah was my friend, and I just wanted to see him outta this system and be a free man."

Just as quick, Tito said, "It don't matter why you did it. You're a good man, KC, and until you prove to me otherwise, you'll always be in my blessings. If you have any problems over this, it won't be because of the money issue. Listen, my people are looking for someone to blame and I'm gonna set the record straight with them, but if one of them walks up on you, it's strictly personal, one-on-one. You do what you gotta do KC, I won't step in."

We extended hands as though we were synchronized and I said, "That's fair, Tito, and I'll pass the word down to my home-boys."

A few months went by with no further words or action, but then out of the blue this dude named Manny Alvarez came into the picture. Apparently, he owed the Hispanics some big money and was approached by the same dude who had come up to me while I was working out. As it turned out, Manny was given a choice- pay up, or take me down, and the debt would be considered paid.

For whatever reason, Manny thought that it would be easier to hit me as opposed to paying off the money he owed to the Hispanics. One day on my way back from work, Manny and I were walking towards each other. As soon as we passed one another, he turned and slashed me across the back with a razor that he had melted onto the handle of a tooth brush *(that was another typical prison weapon)*.

I immediately turned to face him, pulled the shank out of my

184

pocket, and stabbed him in the chest. He then slashed my chest before he took off running towards the stairs. I bolted after him, and as he was trying to get away from me, he fell down the stairs. As soon as he hit the landing, the guards ran up on us. They threw me against the wall, confiscated my shank, handcuffed me, and hauled me off to solitary. Manny went to the hospital. I was charged with another assault and spent several months in solitary awaiting the outcome of the investigation.

While at Leavenworth, I witnessed many things that are unmentionable. I'm not just referring to the inhumane treatment of convicts, but the system's sadistic treatment of the guards as well. A con named J. Moore, who was essentially a drunk, was always fighting with the guards. Everyone, including the prison officials, knew that Moore was a ticking time bomb just waiting to go off. Nonetheless, they instructed a young, inexperienced and cocky guard who had just started at Leavenworth, to go into Moore 's cell and ransack it under the guise that he was looking for contraband.

Everyone, including the Administration, knew that Moore's mother and father had recently died back-to-back, and that the only thing he had left of them were their pictures. So, the guard did as ordered and went into Moore 's cell and threw things everywhere. While he was trashing the cell, the pictures of Moore 's parents fell to the floor. The guard subsequently stepped on them, and left them full of footprints. When Moore got back to his cell, he couldn't see past the trampled pictures of his recently departed parents. As he picked the pictures up from the concrete floor, I saw from my cell that he was trying to wipe them clean. He then stared at the pictures for about 5 minutes, put them down on his bunk, and approached the young guard.

I noticed an eerie calm in his demeanor and instantly knew

185

that the guard was in trouble. As soon as he was within talking distance I heard him ask the guard, "Who searched my cell?" Not knowing the imminent danger he faced, the cocky guard replied, "I did, and what about it?" As if pulling a hankie from his pocket, Moore swiftly pulled his shank out, grabbed the guard by the hair on his head, and decapitated him right there on the spot. As soon as the other guards who were standing nearby realized what had happened, they ran towards Moore as quickly as they could. Without even batting an eye, Moore threw the head at the approaching guards, and then stabbed two of them. For unknown reasons, Moore wasn't sent to solitary, but was instead transferred to the County Jail in Kansas where he mysteriously died shortly after. Although no one 'officially' knows what happened, everyone speculates that the guards killed him.

In prison, no one is safe from the system. Another incident that happened at Leavenworth involved a con named Earl Jones. Earl had killed a few convicts in the past, so he was given several life sentences. That didn't deter Earl, though. Unlike today, there was no death penalty back then, so what they normally did with convicts like Earl was to essentially 'stop' their sentence.

Eventually Earl was reclassified with what's known as a 'P-number' (I guess it's short for PSYCHO) which meant that he was insane and that his sentence remained on hold until the system deemed him sane, (like that would ever happen). Ultimately, there were so many convicts classified with a 'P-number' that they were just intermingled within the general population. Like so many other loonies, Earl had no clue that there was something mentally wrong with him. He would regularly offer to cut someone's hair and would only get about half way through the job before brushing them off and asking "how do you liked your hair cut?" One time, two guys were horse playing and one of them was someone who happened to be good friends with Earl. Earl apparently overheard the other guy say to his 'friend', "Yo. I'm gonna getcha man," so Earl killed the guy later that day. Earl then went back to his friend and said, "Hey, I took care of that for you. " The other convict had no clue what Earl was talking about, so he asked, "Took care of what?" Cool as a cucumber, Earl replied, "You remember that guy you had a problem with today? The one who said that he was 'gonna getcha?' Well I killed him for you. " It never even dawned on Earl that his friend and the other con were actually good friends from way back. So what did Earl get for yet another murder? He received another life sentence, which he continued to serve in general population!

Chapter 18

McNeil Island, WA and Sandstone, MN

Despite it being a case of self-defense at Leavenworth I was found guilty of assault and subsequently sentenced to an additional 5 years. I was also transferred out of Leavenworth and sent to the Federal Prison at McNeil Island, before ultimately being transferred to Sandstone. Although I didn't remain at McNeil very long, I felt like a convict that was confined at Alcatraz, since McNeil and Alcatraz appeared to be built just alike. I was miserable at McNeil. I was surrounded by the ocean, and the weather was always bad. It seemed like it rained every day and every night. When it wasn't raining I was able to go outside to the small yard, but you couldn't even enjoy that because there were thousands of seagulls flying around that would drop their wastes on you. Talk about a feeling of rejection. I remember thinking that I've been kicked off the mainland, and placed out in the ocean where even the birds let you know that they didn't like you and rejected you for being there. I couldn't see anyway of breaking out of that place, so I got into a fight with a guard who tried to take some contraband I had. I was then placed in solitary for a few months and then transferred to Sandstone, Minnesota.

Sandstone is a medium security prison in Minnesota where many " white collar" offenders were sent. It was full of political prisoners, corrupt judges, lawyers, cops, and elderly convicts who spent years in places like Alcatraz and Marion and were no longer

deemed a threat by the system. 'Of all places, why was I sent there?'
I wondered. I eventually heard that the BOP was giving me a last
chance to serve my "ever increasing" time within general
population. Rumor had it that if I couldn't behave in Sandstone, the
BOP was either going to have me institutionalized in an out of state
facility, or have me locked down in solitary for the duration of my
sentence because I was uncontrollable!

Unlike any other place that I'd been incarcerated in,
Sandstone didn't have a perimeter fence! It's an old prison
consisting of multiple buildings that were aligned strategically in a
rectangle to create an outer box. Essentially, the buildings were the
fences and the prison yard was the area located within the walls. I
must admit that being sent to Sandstone was the turning point in my
life. Although seldom the recipient, while at Sandstone I learned
forgiveness, humility and compassion.

Despite the enormous exterior differences of my new
surroundings, I continued to do my time and carry myself as I always
had. Although the majority of the convicts lived within a dorm
setting, as a new arrival I was assigned a single cell within one of
the two cellblocks as opposed to being sent to solitary. I soon
learned that the administration at Sandstone actually had an
'individualized plan' in mind for me. However, since they weren't
sure of the best way to approach me, they sent in the big guns- the
priest and his partner!

Cleverly, Father Boyle called a meeting with the toughest
cons at Sandstone to devise a plan on how to get me to comply with
the 'Father Boyle Behavior Modification Program.' As it turned out,
Father Boyle was better than the administration when dealing with
hard-core convicts. Along with his partner, Honey (a huge German
Sheppard), Father Boyle had won every convict at Sandstone over.

189

He was the most respected man in the joint, and there wasn't a convict there whose heart he didn't own.

I met quite a few notorious cons during my stay at Sandstone. There was Hamilton Sweeney who had spent 13 years in Alcatraz. He was most famous for paralyzing a Jewish gangster while serving time in the Atlanta Federal Prison, but had also stabbed countless other convicts throughout his incarceration. Another con, Bullet, spent 33 years in Alcatraz and was the leader of the Brick Town Rats gang back in the 1920 's and 30 's. He was a stone-cold-killer and bank robber to boot. He was called Bullet because his left arm was paralyzed so he always carried a machine gun in his right hand. There was also a Native American, Ahiga (Navajo for 'he fights'), who was sent to prison for shooting FBI agents at Wounded Knee. Another con was named Gold Tooth. He also served time at Alcatraz, and it was rumored that he completed 50 contracts for the Mafia. I also met Sean Richards, a burglar who made his mark by ripping off the rich and famous during the evening hours. In the long run I became friends with two guys who were key players in the French Connection; Archard and Bayard Claus. Throughout the years their sister Ila visited me as well. It's certainly not an exaggeration to say that while at Sandstone I became well acquainted with numerous people linked to the mob who have since become celebrities.

After about 3 or 4 weeks after being at Sandstone, I was watching a baseball game in the yard when this creepy dude came up beside me. He was dressed in white, and he had his hands stuffed inside of his green coat. As usual, I was always leery of anyone who stood too close or just came up on me, so I kept one eye on the game and the other on this guy.

The fact that I had heard through the grapevine that there was another contract put out on me because of the incident with the Hispanic gang member at Leavenworth didn't help my apprehensiveness towards strangers too much. Of course, it wasn't Tito who had put the hit out on me. He had mysteriously died of a heroin overdose and as a result, the Hispanic gang was in total chaos.

The only thing that I was getting from this mysterious convict were bad vibes. He seemed nervous, as though he were up to something. I kept thinking, 'I don't have any type of weapon on me so if this dude makes a move, I won't stand a chance.' As soon as I saw an opportunity to casually move out of striking distance, I did. As soon as I moved, the dude moved right back next to me. I decided to move again, and so did he! At this point I wasn't worrying about disrespecting anybody, so I just looked at him and said, "What's your problem, dude? Look, if you're part of the hit squad, you should know that I'm unarmed, and the least you could do is tell me what this is all about!"

He slowly pulled his hand out of his pocket and showed me a knife and said, "You're slipping, KC. A convict with your history doesn't come to the prison yard unarmed. As to what this is all about, I'm on a mission for a friend!"

Completely confused at what was going on, I said, "Well, you got me, dude. How come you haven't made your move and are still talking?"

He just shook his head and laughed. So I said, "Okay. I'll bite, what's so funny?" He replied, "Nothing. Now I see what Boyle was talking about."

Totally clueless I asked, "What are you talking about? Who is Boyle?" With a reassuring smile he nodded and answered, "You'll meet him soon enough." Like me, he's a big Irish man. He's also sort

191

of like you, kinda. I hear you're Irish and Indian."

"Yeah, that's right, I'm part Cherokee."

"Well" he said, "One of your Indian brother's is here and wants to meet you. In fact, there are a few of us here who want to get to know you, KC, especially me since your file's almost as bad as mine!"

"So who are you and what's your business?"

"My name's Sweeney, and I've got no business with you. I'm not here to collect on the contract. I came ready for battle because I was warned that you have a proven background of serious violence, and I wasn't going to let you get the upper hand on me. Instead I caught you with your pants down! What's up with that, KC? How come you weren't ready?"

Shrugging my shoulders I said, "I just got here so I haven't had a chance to get ready."

He said, "Look, you're not going to need anything like that here. I only have this knife because I'm getting old and nowadays I can't fight as well as I use to. Laughing, he added, "Besides, I'm not planning on rolling around on the ground with a young dude like you! Anyways, about Boyle - he's actually Father Boyle. He's a real good guy who has taken an interest in you, so he called in the dogs, so to speak. I'm one of the dogs and you'll eventually meet the others."

After putting his knife back in his pocket, he extended his hand to shake mine. As we were shaking hands he asked, "So, are ya ready to meet Boyle?"

"Well, the way I see it I don't have much of a choice, so let's get it over with." Sweeney and I walked over to the prison church and went into the office.

As soon as we walked in, Father Boyle, who was sitting

behind the desk, stood up and reached out his hand. As we were shaking hands he looked over to Sweeney and asked, "Did you have much of a problem in getting him to come here with you?"

Sweeney replied, "I was ready for the worst, but it's been a breeze so far!"

Nodding his head Father Boyle said, "Good then, cause I've got someone else for you to meet, KC, and if you give me any trouble I know he'll take care of ya!"

Now feeling a bit self-conscious I said, "Wait a minute! How come I'm the motion picture here?" Father Boyle replied, "In all honesty, KC, the Warden turned you over to me so I need to make sure that I'm on point when dealing with you."

With no real comeback to his statement, I sat quietly and watched as he walked over to a back door in his office and opened it. To my utmost surprise, out came a big black German Sheppard. He was the most beautiful dog I had ever seen. As soon as he entered the office, he sat right next to Father Boyle. "KC, meet Honey... he's the one who really runs this joint!" Right after the introduction, Honey came over and started sniffing me. A minute later, he barked and started jumping on me while licking my face. I stood up fast as I didn't really know how to handle the situation. Father Boyle and Sweeney sure got a kick out of the whole thing!

Father Boyle looked at me. "Well, now that I see that Honey approves of you, how 'bout you sit back down." As soon as I sat down, Honey came back over and put his paws on me. *I was immediately reminded of the dog that I had as a kid- the one 'that man' threatened to shoot. He would do the same thing every time I sat or lay down, and we would just sit together for hours. I've always loved dogs and truly believe that they are man's best friend.*

"KC, do you like ice cream?" Father Boyle asked.

193

"Yes."

With a smile he said, "So does Honey. As a matter of fact, Honey runs around the whole joint on canteen day because he knows that all the convicts will buy him ice cream and from what I can see here, he'll be running to your cell to collect because he took right to ya'. He usually doesn't take to anyone right away. It usually takes a couple of months before he'll let you touch him. I guess the Warden was wrong about ya' because Honey's approved of you right away and Honey does not like the Warden.

Actually every time the Warden stops by I have to lock Honey up in the next room, which is where we live."

Surprised, I said, "You live inside of this prison?"

Father Boyle replied, "Yes, me and Honey do. So we'll always be here 24 / 7 if you ever need us." Father Boyle then said, "Honey will be around every Sunday morning to make sure you're up and ready for church!"

As I sat there petting Honey, I said, "Father, I'm not really a church person."

"Is that right, KC? Well, then I guess we'll just have to take it one day at a time."

Then I said, "No, really. I don't go to church and to tell ya' the truth Father, for all my life I've been trying to talk to the man upstairs, but He's never answered. As a child I must have done something so horrible that He cast me off completely. It's so bad that sometimes I believe He can't be real and that if He is, He has washed his hands of me."

With a heartrending look, Father Boyle said, "Don't worry, KC, I'm going to talk to Him for you and we're going to try and find out what the problem is." Looking over to Sweeney, he said, "Isn't that right, Sweeney?"

Shaking my head I said, "Look, you don't know me or anything about my past, and if there really was a God, why would He let me suffer the way I have for all of these years?"

Father Boyle answered, "KC, God works in funny ways and I think that He has sent you and the rest of the thugs here to me and Honey for a reason."

Not quite converted by his words I responded, "Look Father, no disrespect intended, but you're wasting your time. I don't want to be a church person. Everything I do is to the best of my ability, be it something good, or bad. Unfortunately, I can't seem to avoid the bad, which means that I would be a hypocrite because on one hand I'd ask the man upstairs for forgiveness and on the other hand, I'm always mixed up in bad things. It's just immoral. The whole thing would just mix me up and if God really does exist, than it would mix Him up, too. I would feel unclean and wicked."

With a kind smile, Father Boyle said, "Thank you, Lord, for giving him to me!"

A bit bothered at this point, I said, "See what I'm saying? You don't know me and you're not listening to me either. You 'God' people are all alike. You all think you have the answers to everyone's problems. I told you that God and I don't talk anymore because He's never answered me. He just ain't listening to me, so I tossed the whole 'God' thing out a long time ago. To this day He's made it perfectly clear to me that I'm on my own in this world. So, Father, be the nice person that I believe you are and just let me do my time. I'll just drop by occasionally to talk with you and see Honey. Besides, I've never lasted in one prison long enough to really get close to anyone. But I really do like your dog. He reminds me of one I once had in my past life."

Nodding his head, Father Boyle looked over to Sweeney and

195

said, "Wow! Does he remind you of anyone?" Laughing Sweeney replied, "Yeah! All of us!"

Father Boyle laughed and said, "Well, KC, let me make a call. I know Bullet, Ahiga, Gold Tooth, and Richards are waiting to come over and they're really anxious to meet you. Is that okay with you?"

In trying to be respectful and get this whole introduction thing over, I replied, "Sure." I figured the sooner they leave me alone, the sooner I can start finding a way outta this place.

Within a few minutes the guys walked in. They all looked like hard-core cons, but each one came over to shake my hand. The last one to walk over was Bullet. Although he also shook my hand, he eyed me from top to bottom. He then looked at Father Boyle and said, "I hate to be the one to tell you this, but he's trouble. I can see it in his eyes- he's pure evil. I wish you all the luck in the world with him Father. Well, I gotta get back to my painting."

As he turned away from Father Boyle, he looked back at me. While shaking his head he said, "damn" as he walked out.

Once he left, the other guys told me not to think negatively about Bullet. They said, "He's an old con and he's seen it all. No one has ever been able to figure him out, nor will he let ya. He's set in his ways and not even a train could move him unless he wanted to be moved. He doesn't talk much to anybody, not even us, so if he ever talks to ya, then you know he likes you."

Sweeney and Gold Tooth also commented that for years Bullet had lived in the cell between both of them while at Alcatraz, and he wouldn't speak to either one of them, let alone look at them. They also noted that for him to look at me in the manner that he did, was unheard of. Then with a nod, Sweeney looked over to Father Boyle and asked, "Don't you think that was pretty odd, Father?"

In agreement Father Boyle also nodded his head and replied, "I would have to certainly agree and quite frankly, I'm wondering what's going on. Not only did he eye KC from top to bottom, but also that's the most I've ever heard him say in the 15 years that he's been here. All he ever does is paint."

Anxious to get outta there I said, "Look guys, I'm not here to judge anyone or try to figure out why that old man doesn't like me or why he would say that I'm evil without even knowing me. To be honest with all of you, I couldn't care less what he or anyone else thinks. All I know is that I have a number just like everyone else in here, and just like everyone else, I've gotta serve my time. So whether anyone likes or dislikes me doesn't matter in the least bit. Although I don't know any of you, I realize that you have all walked your own journey and I respect all of you for that. In turn, I expect all of you to give me my respect as well"

Ahiga immediately replied, "Well put skin," *(skin means Indian brother)* and went on to say, "The spirits brought you to this point in your journey and you can't lead your spirit, you have to let your spirit lead the way. There are likes and dislikes in everyone's journey and why Bullet eyed you in the manner he did, is because he's seen a past vision. He had to set that vision free right away because he didn't like it. Seeing you reminded him of his own journey, both in the past and present."

As if to make light of the moment, the other guys jokingly said, "Ahiga means well, but he sometimes has flashbacks."

Being part Indian myself I replied, "I understand what Ahiga's saying and he's not having flashbacks. What he said is true and I know exactly what he meant"

As Ahiga and I looked at each other and smiled, the other guys said, "Well, we're glad the two of you know what's going on

197

with Bullet!"

Time confirmed that what Bullet saw in me was in fact a vision of a younger Bullet standing before him. Seeing me reminded him of his younger years, and that really scared him. Not that I'm claiming to be another Bullet, but in his mind I was him, and he didn't like looking into his past. Ahiga later told me that he had talked to Bullet about his behavior in Father Boyle's office that day, and that Bullet told him that we had read the whole thing correctly. Ahiga also told me that Bullet would have to come around in order to let both of our spirits face each other, because he was an old evil man who was being eaten alive by his past. He said, "Bullet has to make things right, but he doesn't know how to let go or deal with his past."

From our first meeting, every Sunday I was awakened by either loud licking as Honey drank from the toilet, or by the sound of ripping paper when he looted my canteen for cookies. Father Boyle was determined to get me to church, so he would sneak Honey into my cage every Sunday morning. He knew that Honey reminded me that it was time for me to get outta bed and get to church. Sometimes Honey would even jump into my bunk, which would take me back to when I was a kid and had a dog of my own. Occasionally, I'd get upset with the mess that Honey made in my cage as he ransacked my canteen, but then I heard other cons fussing about the same thing and realized that it was no big deal.

Sunday's weren't as bad as canteen day, however. If Honey didn't have ice cream before entering the cellblock on canteen day, you'd better not be sitting around eating any because he'd run right up on you and take it out of your hand! Some cons got really mad and start cursing at him, but most of them, including me, made sure to always buy ice cream for Honey. It didn't matter where I was in that prison, Honey ALWAYS found me. He'd come sit next to me and nag me until I gave in and played with him.

I couldn't help but think that while I was imprisoned within a cage, here was a dog that has the freedom to go wherever he pleases, yet all that he wants to do is play with a bunch of convicts. Although some of the convicts couldn't care less about the dog, the Warden felt that having him around was a good way of reminding convicts that there's more to life than killing each other. I guess he realized that Honey was capable of bringing happiness into the prison, and especially into the lives of some of the cons.

Even though there were many convicts in Sandstone who hated life as I did, or placed no value on another's, they loved Honey and he owned their hearts. Come to think of it, I wasn't the only one who would have received an assault charge if anyone would have hurt Honey. Despite being authorized by the system to be there, all the cons knew that he wasn't part of the system. They realized that he was totally innocent of his surroundings and the madness that went on around him everyday. I can't help but make a connection between Honey's obliviousness to his surroundings, and those in society who are blind to how the system is treating the human beings within the penal walls before unleashing them back into society.

Unbeknownst to many, I'd say about 75% of all convicts desire a different life than that which was given to them. Unfortunately when they cry out for help, the only one who answers is the system, which pushes their heads back underwater until they can't be heard from again. I've been around enough cons (and some infamous ones too) throughout my life to know that this is true. One convict in particular was a fella outta Milwaukee who had committed some heinous crimes. He was a necrophiliac serial killer and cannibal, who had killed 17 males (mostly children) to prevent

199

them from leaving him. While at the Columbia Correctional Institute in Portage WI, I was confined in the adjoining cage of this infamous killer. Ironically enough, he was killed by a psychotic convict who believed that he was Jesus. Since I couldn't comprehend how another human was capable of taking so many lives, let alone eating another human being, I would often talk with him to try and understand how his mind worked.

One of the first things he made me understand was that too often, parents neglect (either intentionally or unintentionally) their children because of their hectic lives. He told me that most, if not all of his victims, were estranged from their families, or like in my case, abandoned. He would tell me about his childhood and how his own parent's neglect had turned him into the killer he had become. Not once did he try to minimize his crimes, or deflect the blame of his actions onto others. After talking with him personally, I've come to the conclusion that he too had become a product of his past.

After his murder, I heard that his brain had been donated to science so they could figure out why he had become a monster. The death of this convict is just another example of how the system plays an active role in deciding who gets to live and who dies. I could never figure out how society considered him sane enough to imprison him. Although I'll be the first to admit that it's been over 40 years since I've lived among the general public, when did society deem it 'normal' to have sex with corpses, eat humans, and want to create zombies?

Before his death, we would spend countless hours talking. One particular day while in the rec yard, we were talking about how some of the other convicts were calling him names and telling him that they were going to kill him as soon as they got the chance. Shaking his head, he just looked at me with a very sincere look in his

eyes and said, "KC, I don't know why these guys hate me so much.
We're all in here for the same thing." It was at that moment that I
realized that he didn't deem his crimes atrocious. He had no clue
that his crimes were beyond those committed by 'normal' people. In
his mind, he didn't consider himself any different than any other
murderer and sincerely thought that his crimes were no worse than
anyone else's.

Another conversation we had which has always stuck with
me had to do with brick acid. He told me that you could place a body
inside of a barrel with brick acid, and a week or two later you could
easily flush all of the contents down the drain or toilet.

Although it's my understanding that there were 17 victims,
after hearing that story I honestly wondered just how many innocent
children actually suffered a terrible death at his hands. Thinking
about it today makes me just as sick, just as it did when I spoke with
him through the fence all those years ago. He even told me how he
would drill holes into his victim's skulls so that he could pour acid
into their heads so they would become powerless, giving himself full
control. In all honesty, that conversation reminded me of the penal
system and how it would get its hold on those convicts who never
had anything in their lives. The system would render them powerless
and allow the most vulnerable convicts to be victimized so that
others could attain the trophy of 'jailhouse respect'; much in the
same way this monster viewed his form of control as a trophy that he
could claim as his own.

Although I'm no expert, the bottom line is that serial killers
aren't created from being dropped on their head as a child.
Throughout my incarceration, I have met several serial killers and
even shared a cage with a few of them. Of all the serial killers I've
met, the most dangerous dudes are the ones who have been created

and nurtured within the penal system. Ticking like a time bomb waiting to explode, they're the ones who haven't started killing yet. The ones who with every passing day, swallow their rage and wait for the day when they will be released back into society. They yearn to unleash the pain and suffering inflicted upon them by the system. When society turns a blind eye to child abuse, why isn't it held accountable for not taking action to make sure that a serial killer doesn't emerge? I hope someday to be able to help educate the general public about the myriad of convicts that are incarcerated for non-homicidal crimes (theft, drug trafficking, assault) and evolve into serial killers within the penal walls. Society must ensure that non-violent prisoners are segregated from the hard-core convicts, and needs to realize as long as it doesn't hold itself accountable for what happens to those it incarcerates, it can't realistically expect those who walk out of their correctional facilities to be undamaged human beings who have learned their lesson. Society should also be watchful of how its tax dollars are being spent by the Prison Systems.

I know first hand that many cons believe society regards them as worthless, and has cast them into the pits of hell to be forgotten. From the convict's point of view, society is simply seeking revenge for their crimes, and that whatever happens to them while they are incarcerated is justly deserved. Regrettably, society is biased and inclined to measure every crime with the same ruler. By turning their backs on those they condemned, society has endorsed the abuse and torture that goes on behind the penal walls in the name of 'rehabilitation'. Nowadays, all you hear about is the abuse going on at military prisons like Guantanamo Bay, and all the investigations into the allegations made by former prisoners. This is going on in all of the United States' prisons, but no one's talking or doing anything about it. It is shocking that society wonders why so many convicts come out worse than when they went in.

With the assistance of his persistent partner Honey, Father Boyle finally got me to go to church. I wasn't then, nor am I now, one to outwardly voice my opinion about God and whether or not He exists. But over time, I came to understand that not only is He real, but also that He has been in my life for all of these years. Father Boyle helped me to understand that if it had not been for God, I wouldn't be here today. Throughout all these years, God has given me the strength to endure the hardships of my journey.

It was while I was at Sandstone that I believed enough in God to ask him for a Christian woman. I had heard from several of the other convicts that Christian women stood by your side no matter what the circumstances, although I knew that some of the cons were only after the materialistic gains that a Christian woman might be able to offer. Some even felt that Christian women were more vulnerable and easier to manipulate than other women, and could easily be swindled out of money. Even though I wasn't a Christian, I always felt it was shameful to use another for self gain. I only wanted a woman to become *one* with. As years went by, many women visited me in prison, but my heart never felt the true meaning of love. While most of them were nice, there wasn't that *spark* between us that was needed to take the relationship beyond that of just a friendship. Unbeknownst to me at the time, there was a wonderful woman many miles away from Sandstone who was asking for the same thing.

She prayed to God that He would bring her a man to be her husband and soul mate. All I can say now is 'God is good'. As I moved on with my time at Sandstone, I was assigned to work in the print shop. I learned the printing trade and actually enjoyed the work.

The only thing that stood in my way of progressing was the lack of education I had. However, I refused to accept the fact that I needed an education. By becoming a ward of the state at such a young age, and from being institutionalized throughout the typical school years, I convinced myself that rudimentary skills such as reading and writing were only needed in 'real life.'

I learned how to compensate for my ignorance in certain situations and avoided having to answer simple math or spelling questions. I even believed that since I had bought a G.E.D. at Leavenworth for a carton of cigs that I really didn't need to know how to read or write. All I had to do was provide proof of a G.E.D. to get the job, and then use my common sense to learn the task. Heck, as far as I was concerned once you're in the door, who needed an education? Year after year I heard convicts whine about how they couldn't get a job because they didn't have a G.E.D. and all I could think was 'how dumb- use your head and buy one!' Man, did I get a rude awakening years later.

One day I went over to the hobby room to see some of Bullet's artwork. Convicts were always raving about his artwork and talking about how he painted with just one arm so I had to go see it for myself. As soon as I stepped into the hobby room and saw his art, I thought it was breathtaking. I had never seen such beautiful art before. Even though I dabbled a bit in Native American drawings, I felt about art as I did an education- who needs to be an artist? But Bullet's work was inspiring. Cons stood and looked at his paintings for hours on end.

Oddly though, Bullet knew that I was there to see his artwork, but he never even looked at me or said a word as if I was invisible. I really wanted to ask him about his artwork and wanted to know why he became an artist and what his inspiration was. Since I was just as stubborn as he was, I never initiated a conversation. However, I did make it a point to stop by the hobby shop every night for about an hour or so to watch him paint. Every now and then Bullet would scan the room to see who was watching, and every time he looked over towards me or even came my way I would just turn around and leave.

One night as I was walking away, I looked back and saw him smiling. As soon as our eyes met, he dropped his smile and put his convict frown back on. That night, I was the one eyeing him from top to bottom and when I finally decided to turn back around and walk away, I heard someone call out, "KC!"

At first I thought I was hearing things so I just kept walking, but then I heard my name again. Completely shocked, I turned back towards him and asked, "Did you call me?"

"I usually only call someone once, and if they don't hear me than I never call again."

Coolly I said, "Well I wasn't sure that I heard correctly."

With a nod he said, "I've been watching you come down here every night for months now, so do you like art, or are you just hoping that I'll talk with you?"

"I have heard what a good artist you are, so I wanted to come see it for myself. And yes, I've always liked art although I'm no artist. Insofar as you speaking to me, I couldn't care less if you ever directed a word my way. Your art's enough for me."

With his usual hard-nosed look he replied, "Had you of answered that question any other way I would have told you to get lost and stay away from my work area." The greatest shock of all came shortly after when he asked, "Do you wanna learn how to paint?" Quicker than the bat of an eye I replied, "Sure! I'd like to learn to paint!"

205

"Well, go over to that locker next to mine and pull out your supplies. Set up the easel right here next to me so we can get started."

As soon as I opened the locker that he pointed to, I saw a nametag with 'KC' on it. I then focused on all the supplies inside of the locker, which I knew were worth a few hundred dollars. I turned back toward him and said, "Bullet, I know there's hundreds of dollars worth of supplies here- how can I pay you back since I don't have any money?"

With an unfamiliar carefree look he replied, "I want your first painting, and I want you to give me your word that you won't stop painting, no matter how bad your artwork is at first."

While I stood silently thinking about the commitment I was about to make he said, "You'd better think hard about my conditions, KC, because I don't like cons that give me their word and then go back on it."

Without further thought, I was ready. "Bullet, I give you my word that as long as I have access to art materials, I will never stop painting!"

As an acknowledgment of my pledge Bullet said, "Okay, then. You just bought yourself lessons and art supplies. And by the way, if you would have given me your word without much thought I would have told you to leave. You've proven to be a smart boy, KC."

It was 1975 when I first sat down next to Bullet to begin my painting lessons. He started me out by painting some of the most famous clowns in the world. After a year of sitting next to Bullet he looked over to my canvas and said, "That one."

Unclear as to what he was talking about I asked, "What do you mean?" "I meant a year ago that the first painting that I liked was mine, so I want that one."

I was happy to say, "Alright, then Bullet. This one's yours!"

Seemingly full of pride, he told me, "You're an artist now, KC. You've been able to paint everything I've set before you, so your lessons are over. You're on your own now kid, just like you were when you first came into this world."

As we laughed at his analogy I told him that he was the best teacher I'd ever had. With a half smile he responded, "No, KC. You've always had it in you to be an artist. You just needed a little help to bring it out."

After that day, Bullet and I ate and walked the prison yard together everyday for 2 years. Throughout all that time, the other cons (along with Father Boyle and the Warden) just couldn't figure out how such a hardened old convict like Bullet could become best friends with me.

One specific day while we were taking a smoke break, Bullet was covered in paint and holding his paint brush. He was having a tough time trying to light his cigarette with a brush in his hand, so I pulled out a pack of matches and lit one to help him out. As I moved the lit match toward his cigarette, he blew it out and said, "If we were in the woods and took a crap and couldn't wipe my butt, would you wipe it for me?"

Without any hesitation I yelled, "Hell no, I wouldn't wipe your old butt!"

"Then don't help me light my smoke."

Shaking my head I said, "You know Bullet, you're an old angry man and you should be glad that I put up with your comments because no one else will. That's why all the other cons stay away, man."

Grinning from ear to ear he said, "Is that right boy? So how does it feel to see yourself in about 40 years?"

Staring back at him, I thought back to that first day we met in Father Boyle's office and at how hard he had looked at me. I also thought of Ahiga's remark of how Bullet had seen himself in me. In an attempt to just dismiss the whole conversation I said, "Well Bullet, it's lunch time so let's go eat."

"I guess that means you don't have anything else to say, huh, KC?"

As I put my hand on his shoulder I said, "Come on old man. Let's go." As we walked back towards the mess hall, I continued talking. "You know, I wondered why you looked at me so hard the first time we met."

Shrugging his shoulders he asked, "What does that have to do with anything?"

"I reminded you of yourself when you were my age in prison. I understand you, Bullet, and it doesn't matter to me how mean you are because I know who you are and how you feel based on my own experiences in life."

Bullet and I never spoke about that day. During our friendship he told me that he dreamed of opening an art gallery in Minnesota once he was released and in time his dream came true, but he died shortly afterwards of natural causes. That was *38* years ago and to this day I haven't stopped painting. (You can see some of my paintings in the back of the book)

As my time continued at Sandstone, I came across a few more interesting cons. Two that I became friendly with were the Claus brothers who were the ones linked to the French Connection. Bayard (one of the two brothers) was that first one that I met. He was a key player in the illegal money making business. Although he was young, rich and full of street smarts, he was dim-witted when it came to the prison system, which made him vulnerable to the hard-core convicts. I met him in the prison yard one day as I was working out. While he watched me work out, I already knew the low down on him. I knew who he was, why he was in prison, and the length of his sentence (actually he had a relatively short sentence of only 3 years.) I stopped working out for a minute and said, "It's Bayard, right?" He replied that it was. With such a short response I asked, "Well, do ya wanna work out?"

"Yeah I would like to start, but I need someone to show me how."

Acknowledging his request for help, I told him to come on over, and we started to walk the yard together. As we walked, he told me why he was in prison. He told me about his family and how they owned a shoe store chain, and how he had come from money. He also told me that he was scared and lost inside prison, and that he didn't think he would make it to see the end of his sentence. His words and sincerity reminded me about how I felt when I first entered the adult system. As we walked further, I thought to myself that I had to try to do what I could for this guy to help get through the short sentence he had. A short time later, Bayard informed me that he had told his wife that we were friends, and that his wife wanted to meet me. I added her to my visit list.

Within a week or so, Bayard and I walked out to the 'visitor's hall' together and although she was very nice and we had a good time, it was really hard for me to be around people from the *free* side of the walls. For some reason I always felt outta place, but I enjoyed talking with her and she always brought me something to eat, so I did the best I could to cope. During one visit she thanked me for befriending Bayard during this time in his life and told me that she could see that he was doing better. *I don't know if she ever knew this, but at one point Bayard even talked about killing himself. I told*

209

him that I didn't want to hear that kind of talk from him, or I would walk away from our friendship. I also told him that he had to bite the bullet and just do his time so that he could go home.

Apparently, Bayard also told his sister Ila about our friendship, and that she also wanted to meet me. I added her to my visit list as well. She started visiting me and we quickly became friends. *It was really nice meeting people in Bayard's family- they made me feel as though someone cared about me too.* Before we knew it, Bayard made parole, but before he left he came to me and said, "KC, I need you to do one more thing for me."

I asked, "What's that?" He said "My brother, Archard, will be coming in to serve his 3 years for his role in the French Connection, and I need you to look out for him like you did with me. He'll never make it in here without your help. He'll be coming in a couple of weeks."

To try and make light of the situation and ease his worries I smiled and said, "Wow, man. I just walked you through this nightmare and now I have to do it all over again for your brother? I don't know if I can deal with another one like you!"

Obviously uptight about the whole thing, he didn't understand that I was joking so he replied, "I'll pay you, KC."

Shaking my head, I reassuringly put my hand on his shoulder and said, "Man, I was just kidding."

Now nodding his head in acknowledgement of my intent he asked, "Well, then what can I do for you when I get out, KC?"

I replied, "Nothing dude, I don't need anything." Then as an after thought I said, "Wait. Actually there is something you can do for me."

Eagerly he replied, "What is it, KC? Anything that I can do for you, I will. Just name it." So I said, "When you leave this hell hole take that crazy sister of yours with ya and keep her away- she's driving me nuts!"

We both burst out laughing and I said, "Just kidding about your sister, but there really is one thing you, your wife and Archard can do for me before he comes in."

Again Bayard didn't hesitate. "Just name it, KC!"

"The day you're paroled, I want your wife to pick you up in a long, black limousine and I want Archard to be the chauffer. I want him to get out of the limo, and while sporting the whole chauffer uniform, open the door for your wife and help her out. When she gets out, I want to see her outfitted in a long dark dress, holding two champagne glasses. I also want to see you dressed in a nice black suit. When you walk up to the car I want you both to lock arms, and toast to freedom. Before you get into the car I want you to salute the gun tower, give him the 'finger', and then drive away."

Looking at me strangely he asked, "You really want that, KC?"

I replied, "Yes. That would make my day!"

Shrugging his shoulders he said, "Okay, you got it. But why would you ask for something like that when I'm offering you *anything* you want?"

I replied, "Because I can't do it, and I've been dreaming of doing it for years. My only way of sharing your freedom is for you to *flip them the bird* from the other side of the wall."

Nodding, he responded, "Okay, KC. No problem- you got it".

The day before Bayard was paroled, I got Bullet, Sweeney, Ahiga, Richards, Gold Tooth and a couple other old-timers together and informed them of what Bayard would be doing the next morning. When I gave them the details of my request, they all said

211

that Bayard wouldn't do it. I insisted that he would, and that I needed them to be with me in the morning watching out the window to witness the moment.

Although skeptical, they came with me in the morning and much to their surprise, a limousine pulled up to the gate. Sure enough, out came Bayard's brother, Archard, dressed in uniform. He walked to the passenger door and let out Bayard's wife. She was dressed in the most beautiful evening dress that I had ever seen. As soon as she stepped out from the limo, the catcalls started. We all watched in envy as Bayard (also dressed nicely) walked over to his wife and made their toast. However, the best part was when all three of them faced the gun tower and on cue, flipped the gun tower guard the bird! The only thing missing was being able to see the guard's face as he watched the whole thing go down.

I later got the chance to ask the guard on duty that day what he thought. With a smile, he shook his head and said, "I've never seen anything like it." I had no choice, but to laugh about the whole thing."

Even Father Boyle had witnessed the whole thing, and told us that he also enjoyed the performance, but that the finger part could have been left out. Then he looked at me and shook his head.

A week after Bayard Claus was paroled, his brother, Archard, turned himself in and walked into Sandstone. We quickly picked up where Bayard and I left off- working out and walking the yard together. Just like Bayard, Archard was a good person and apparently possessed more 'book smarts' than Bayard. I quickly figured that he was the mastermind behind their *operation* on the street. Similar to Bayard, Archard did everything he could to help me from the other side of the wall and promised me that if and when I got outta prison, he and his family would help me in everyway possible.

The Claus brothers, along with their immediate family, lived up to their promise. For many years they sent me money and other essential items. Even after I had asked them to stop, they continued to send me gifts. I guess they ignored my request because they felt that that was the only way to help me through to the next day in hell.

As one might expect, Archard was assigned to work in the print shop with me and was instantly shown respect because of my status. One morning as we were walking to work, a con completely engulfed in flames ran past us. Archard had never really been exposed to prison violence, so the site of a convict on fire petrified him.

As it turned out, that incident wasn't an act of prison violence but was instead self-inflicted. The convict was actually one of the 'Eight' (military draft dodgers) and by what we later heard, he was the only one not granted parole, so he poured gasoline on himself and lit a match.

As he ran past us screaming, he apparently succumbed to the pain a few yards away and fell to the ground. When Archard and I came up on him, the only things left burning were his prison boots. He was completely charred, and unrecognizable as a person. As I looked over to Archard, I saw him bent over, vomiting his entire breakfast. I walked over to him and said, "Come on, man. Let's get outta here before the guards show up."

As soon as we got to the print shop, Archard went straight to the bathroom to clean himself up. When he came out he walked over to me and said, "KC, I don't know how you deal with this type of stuff."

Genuinely unaffected by what we had just witnessed, I calmly replied, "Archard, I have been forced to deal with this

213

environment during most of my childhood and throughout my entire adult life. Unfortunately here, life just moves forward and you try not to look back and hope that nothing happens to you."

Clearly traumatized by the incident and visibly shaking, he said, "I've never seen anything like that in my whole life", and I replied "well, just hang in there- hopefully you'll be going home soon and you won't have to worry about these things ever again." As Archard's time to going home grew nearer, I was sent into the State System, and transferred to Waupun, WI to start my 0 - 20 year sentence for a bank robbery that I committed while a fugitive of the Federal System.

Within a few weeks after leaving Sandstone, Archard made parole. Although we haven't seen each other since, I phoned him about 14 years ago. He told me that once he re-entered society, he changed his name just like his brother Bayard had done. They decided to start a home-based business. Unfortunately, his brother and he were ambushed a few years earlier and Bayard was murdered. Archard escaped alive, but was confined to a wheelchair for life. On the day I called Archard, he was getting ready to go to Mexico for a vacation. With all sincerity he asked me if I'd like to join him on his next one, but I had to tell him that I wouldn't be on the other side of the fence for a long, long time. We wished each other well, and that was the last time we talked.

Chapter 19

Waupun, WI

Little did I know at that time, Waupun would change my life forever. It was at Waupun that I married and divorced my second wife, Susan. *Susan worked for the Wisconsin Department of Corrections when we met. Over the years during my time at Waupun, we eventually became close friends and decided we wanted to get married. Soon afterwards, Susan transferred out of Corrections and took a job at the University of Wisconsin so that there were no conflicts with the penal system, and we could move forward with our lives. Around the same time that we got married, I was scheduled to go before the Wisconsin Parole Board. Unfortunately for me, the Director of the Parole Board (who I later found out was in love with Susan) denied me any relief for parole which eventually lead to our divorce. Needless to say, marrying Susan was held against me in the worst way.*

While at Waupun, I prevented an attack against a group of children who were coming into the prison as part of a 'Get Straight' program. I saved several lives that day, including that of a guard's. One of the most powerful white cliques was planning on shooting the tour guard, and then taking the children hostage. It was rumored that they intended to mutilate and kill the children if the Administration didn't agree to their various demands, which included the immediate improvement of conditions within the prison. At the time I was working as a tier rep, (back then I was called a 'cell hall clerk') and heard about the plan through the grapevine and how it was all supposed to go down. Knowing what I did, I was compelled to do something. I absolutely could not let innocent children walk into a trap- especially knowing the fate that awaited them if the clique were to successfully carry out their plan.

That morning I went to the visit hall to see Susan (by this time we were divorced, but remained friends). As soon as Susan saw me she asked, "What's wrong KC? You look a bit agitated."

I replied, "I am Sue. I know how to deal with these hard core cons, but I can't jump ugly with them without them taking me down first."

Confused by what I had just said she asked, "What are you talking about?"

I calmly told her about what the clique was planning on doing later that day, and asked her what she thought I should do. She grabbed my hand and said, "If you're the man that I know you are, you'll prevent this whole thing from happening. Can't you go talk to them?"

Shaking my head I said, "No, they won't listen to me on this one. Those cons have their mind set on getting what they want and if that means killing a guard and some kids... they're gonna do it."

She squeezed my hand and said, "KC, think about those kids. Remember how scared you were all those times when you were put in danger?"

Acknowledging what she said I replied, "You're right Susan, I can't let this go down. Let's cut our visit short so that I can get back to the cell block."

We hugged each other harder than ever before, and I kissed her goodbye. I watched as she left the visitor's hall, and made sure she was through the gates before I headed back to the unit. Since most of the clique members were still visiting, I slipped into the clique leader's cell and grabbed the sack that they were using to keep the gun and knives inside of. I immediately took it to the front of the cellblock where Sgt. Kane had already started letting the kids in. I grabbed his arm and pulled him close to me, shoved the sack in his hand and said in his ear, "Take this and get out of the cellblock now. Make sure those kids go with you."

Alarmed by my actions, he turned away from the kids and looked in the sack. He then turned back towards me and asked, "What the hell's going on, KC?"

I leaned towards him and said, "Kane, they're about to take over the cellblock and they're planning on killing you. Then they're gonna take the kids hostage and torture them, to death if need be, unless the Administration gives them what they want. Save your life and those kids by leaving now!"

With terror in his eyes he said, "Man, thank you."

I pushed him out the door and pulled it shut, which automatically locked behind him. Less than a minute later, I saw everyone coming back from the visitor's hall and noticed the clique leader rushing back into his cell. I watched as he emerged from his cell. As he came out, he started to look around the cell and noticed me standing there alone. He immediately walked towards me and asked, "Where's the guard and the 'Get Straight' kids? What's going on? Why are you here alone?"

By this time, all of his homeboys were behind him, so I just looked at the dude and simply replied, "It's over man. Even though I didn't have anything to do with your plan, I couldn't let you hurt those kids. I gave Kane your weapons and pushed him and the kids outta the cell block. I didn't give him any names and he has no idea about whose plan it was. What was about to go down is something

217

that I couldn't live with, so I had to put a stop to it. I know I'm a convict just like you and your homeboys, but I'm not an animal, I'm a human being."

One of his homeboys said, "You're a dead man, KC!"

Even though I knew that they didn't have any knives on them, I knew that I was in grave danger. They all rushed towards me, and I was able to get a couple of hits in before hitting the floor. They over powered me quickly, and beat me viciously until they saw the guards coming. As soon as the guards reached the gate, everyone immediately retreated into their cells. I was rushed to the hospital and as soon as I was able to travel, I was transferred out of Waupun.

My time within the Wisconsin Prison System had finally come to an end. Susan divorced me years ago because of the life I was forced to endure, along with her sense of helplessness regarding the injustices against me. Unbeknownst to us when we were married, we were not destined to be life-long soul mates. That wasn't the plan for us. However, she had to be in my life at a specific time.

Chapter 20

Green Bay, WI

I was sent to Green Bay State Prison, where I quickly learned that the cons back in Waupun wanted me dead. According to the stories I heard, they weren't publicizing that they planned on killing innocent children, but they sure were spreading the word that I had badly 'disrespected' them. Unsurprisingly, my time at Green Bay wasn't easy. Even so, I was able to accomplish a few things in the 14 years or so that I was incarcerated there.

Primarily, I was able to overcome my self-imposed barrier of illiteracy. Not only did I 'legitimately' earn my G.E.D., but I also attended college. *I must admit that initially I gave the folks at Green Bay a copy of the G.E.D. that I had bought at Leavenworth. That worked great for a while until some of the cons in the wood factory wanted my friend and I, Johnny Bricks, to go work with them. (Not only would we make better wages, but we would also all be able to hang out together.) Johnny and I told them that we couldn't pass the math test that was required, and since they knew all about 'buying' an education in prison, they offered to tutor us. (Little did they know that not only were we lacking in math, but we couldn't even spell our names!)*

Within a few days, the guys taught us the basics and even gave us a 'cheat sheet' for the more difficult problems. Ready to take the test, Johnnie and I went to the office and sat down next to each other. Wouldn't you know it, the guy who was administering the test sat down right in front of me. As soon as he told us to begin the test, I started to sweat because I wasn't going to be able to use my 'cheat sheet'. I was so preoccupied with him sitting in front of me that I completely forgot everything the guys had taught me! Frustrated by the whole thing I said, "Look man, I can't take this test but if you put me out on the floor I assure you that I can hold my own."

Johnny quickly said, "Me, too."

Surprisingly, with a tone of encouragement he looked at both of us and replied "I bet you both could, but I would be doing you an injustice if I did that. I promise you that if you two attend classes and pass your G.E.D., I'll hire the both of you. "

Johnny and I acknowledged his terms, and left the office mad as hell. As we walked back to the cellblock, Johnny asked me what I was going to do. Shaking my head in disgust I told him that I was tired of being dumb and that I was going to go to school. Once again, he said, "Me, too," and we signed up for classes. We were so behind that we had to start out in the special-ed level, but hey- where there's a will, there's a way! Not only did we get the job in the wood factory, but the next time we both went before the Parole Board and were asked what we had done for ourselves, we proudly informed them that we had earned our G.E.D.

In hindsight that wasn't a good idea because both of us were denied parole for committing fraud with the Leavenworth paperwork. I guess honesty is not always the best policy!

I was involved in quite a few fights at Green Bay as a result of my moral judgment at Waupun. Despite my nobleness, I was ultimately sent to solitary for defending myself against those who were trying to 'move up the ranks' within the prison. While in solitary, there was a guard who obviously wanted to show-off in front of the female guard that he was training. One day, he decided to impress her by kicking the food trap in my cell door shut while I was reaching for the tray. Needless to say, I was left with a broken hand. I was completely denied any medical assistance, so my hand had to heal on its own. As soon as the opportunity presented itself, I stabbed the guard who assaulted me. Consequently, I was sent to Marion, which is the super-max facility that replaced Alcatraz.

It might sound cold-blooded that I stabbed that guard, but if you were forced to 'live in my shoes' under those conditions that I was forced to live under for so many years, you may have done the same thing. Later on in life, I was informed that I suffered from Post Traumatic Stress Disorder (PTSD). I was told that my PTSD was caused by traumatic experiences from incarceration, and long-term institutional abuse. Sufferers deal with intense psychological distress, along with physiological reactivity when exposed to such triggering memories of the institutional abuse. The affected also suffer from dissociation, emotional numbing, and many chronic problems with their mental functions that include irritability, outbursts of anger, difficulty concentrating, and sleep disturbances. Another symptom of PTSD is an exaggerated startle response as a result of the persistent avoidance of anything that would trigger memories of the traumatic events in the past and present. This can also be related to a constant state of hypervigilance, generalized paranoia, and a truly reduced capacity to trust anyone caused by a constant fear of abuse from both correctional staff and other inmates.

No human being should ever be forced to endure the conditions as expressed within the covers of this book, and I pray that God will give me the opportunity upon my release to assist all who are concerned to end such treatment in institutions.

221

Chapter 21

Marion, IL

Since Marion is essentially a 'long-term solitary confinement' facility with a 'First-Aid' level medical unit, only convicts considered in good health (i.e., no one requiring any type of medication) were accepted by Marion's Administration. At Marion, you're 'locked-down' for 23 hours a day and denied any type of human contact. *I truly believe that circus animals are treated more humanely.*

At Marion, you are systematically dehumanized. The weak-minded convicts end up committing suicide, while the strong-minded are either killed by the guards, or worse, endure dismal years of torturous solitude in an oppressive cage. Marion even had an in-house court system where judges were brought in when needed so that the convicts had absolutely no reason to ever leave the grounds. Marion was also notorious for trumping up 'institutional or administrative' charges against defiant convicts. This meant that if a convict survived their bid and had as little as 1 day left in their sentence, the administration would *intervene* and reset their sentence. As an example, if a convict entered Marion with a 10-year sentence and had served 9 years and 363 days, on the 364th day a guard would find or fabricate a reason to charge him and essentially cancel out all of the time that he had already served. *Unbelievably outrageous right? Well, it happens more often than people are willing to admit.*

Despite Marion's strict 'good health' criteria, I noticed that quite a few convicts around me were quite sick. As a matter of fact, a convict that had apparently finished up his solitary confinement was escorted by a couple of guards into the cell right next to me. As I looked at him, he appeared to be very ill and even looked yellow. After the guard left, I asked him where he was just transferred from and he told me he had been in Marion for several years serving his solitary bid and he was being transferred to another federal prison where he would be placed into general population.

Being that he looked so sick, I said. "Really? You don't look well enough to even be here." He told me that he was fine when he arrived at Marion, but that over the years he hadn't been feeling well and he kept getting worse as the time went by. He then told me something that really freaked me out. He told me that it wasn't uncommon for those convicts who came to Marion because of an assault on a guard, or who were considered a threat to the system, to become extremely ill before being transferred. He said the convicts that didn't die or become paralyzed were diagnosed with a number of health problems upon leaving. Apparently, his theory was that those convicts were purposely made sick somehow by the administration at Marion. He told me he believed he was infected with something, and that he was awaiting a copy of his medical records, which he requested through the FOIA (Freedom Of Information Act), to prove that he was fine before he was transferred to Marion

Then I thought to myself, 'Wait a minute... I haven't been feeling very well lately, I'm here because of a guard assault, and I'm suppose to be transferred out soon as well.'

After about a minute I dismissed his theory as extreme paranoia and said, "Well I sure am glad that they haven't given me anything!" A few days later, the sick convict banged on my wall and said, "Hey KC, I just got my records and you've gotta check this out."

He handed me a paper with *my name* on it, which read, "Chronic Hepatitis B & C. Needs to be seen by a liver specialist". In total disbelief I told him to stop messing around because I knew that he didn't have access to my file. With a very serious tone, he told me that he would never joke about something like that. He told me that they had made a huge mistake and mixed my records in with his. He asked me if they had done any blood work on me recently. I told him that they had indeed done blood work on me in order to clear me for a transfer since I hadn't been feeling well lately. I informed him that I was told by the staff that everything was okay and that I probably just had some bug, so they gave me some cold medicine.

He said, "Well if I were you, KC, as soon as I got to where I was going, I'd drop a slip to see a doctor. Obviously something' s not right here." From Marion I was transferred to Florence; another super max prison.

Although I've lost the exact count, I know I've spent a total of about 20 years in solitary confinement since 1961. For all intents and purposes, Marion and Florence are 'the end of the line'. You only make it out of those facilities one of two ways - through the grace of God, or in a body bag.

Amnesty International Questionnaire on Torture and Ill Treatment
(Submitted in February 2000)

PLEASE FILL OUT THE QUESTIONNAIRE AS COMPLETELY AS YOU CAN AND RETURN IT DIRECTLY TO AMNESTY

Dear Amnesty,

My wife, Mrs. J Amos called your office on 01/31/2000, and explained to whom she talked with that I was placed into an institution at the age of 10 years old, and that I am now 49 years old. I have been incarcerated for approximately 38 years for crimes of theft, escapes, and issues based on my being confined as a child and into my adulthood, and didn't have an adult sentence until I escaped from federal prison in 1971. Your office then sent my wife this questionnaire for me to fill out and return, and we are praying that God will touch your hearts to help us receive some relief.

1. PLEASE GIVE YOUR NAME AND MAILING ADDRESS AT THE DETENTION CENTER OR PRISON

Danny Lee Amos; Housed by State and Federal Prisons, and numerous other prisons in the United States.

2. DESCRIPTION OF TORTURE OR ABUSE: WHEN DID THE INCIDENT TAKE PLACE? WHAT HAPPENED DURING THE INCIDENT AND WHO TOOK PART IN IT? WERE THERE OTHER WITNESSES TO THE INCIDENT? DID YOU SUSTAIN ANY INJURIES, AND IF SO, DID YOU

RECEIVE MEDICAL TREATMENT?

From age ten into my adulthood while incarcerated, I have suffered years of solitary confinement under the worst conditions that most human beings couldn't endure let alone comprehend the torture and abuse. The following is a list of the torture and abuse I have suffered for several years.

At age ten I was placed naked in a solitary confinement cell, beaten by detention home staff, and left in those conditions for weeks at a time. While confined in institutions I suffered beating after beating by the staff. I endured abuse such as water being placed on my back, being bent over and having my head locked between the staff person's legs. He would start high in the air with his arm and come down hard as he could with the open hand numerous times against my back which would leave a handprint in my back for days.

I was made to chew lye soap until I could blow a bubble; the lye soap caused my gums to be raw for days. I was beaten numerous times on the top of my head with a wooden oak block triangle that had the staff's name on it, during which I had to thank the staff person for abusing me. This left large knots and cuts on my head. I've had my head pushed between the two hands of staff members into a wooden locker edge, which being very sharp caused open gashes in my head. I've endured the staff taking the end of a pocketknife and banging it into the top of my head numerous times. I've been tied to a flagpole and beaten with what they called a *cat of nine tails* on my bare back for the whole institution to see. A cat of nine tails was made of strips of leather with knots tied into each strip. The strips were connected to a leather handle that was used to hit me numerous times, causing scars on my back that I still have today.

I was placed into a solitary cell with no lights at all, just a hole in the floor for bodily wastes. I was given an army blanket to sleep on a concrete floor for months at a time. Rats would come up out of the waste hole in the floor and try to get next to my body to keep warm. I would have to use my teeth and bite the edge of the blanket until I could tear strips away. I would then bite holes down both sides of the blanket so I could use the strips and sew the blanket together to make a gunnysack that I could crawl inside so the rats wouldn't touch my skin.

While in this solitary cell, I was forced by the staff to have a metal spoon placed in my mouth and forcibly shoved down my throat in order to stop me from complaining about my conditions. When the spoon went down my throat, I couldn't breathe. My throat was moved by the staff's hands to make me swallow. During this incident I was even rushed to a hospital and under went surgery to remove the spoon. This took place in the Missouri Prison System.

I was housed in a cellblock where the cells didn't have a sink or any fixtures for bodily wastes. I was given a large coffee can to use for my waste during the night. Inmates were forced to fight each other for the amusement of the staff. I was forced to stand in one spot, bent over, holding my ankles for hours. If I fell over or moved in the slightest, I was beaten. I was worked from sun up until sun down in the worst conditions imaginable. I forced myself to endure the harsh conditions because of the fear of being tortured. It is very hard for an outsider to comprehend the torture and abuse that we endured.

The incidents stated above took place in various institutions in the state of Missouri, when I was between 10 and 15 years of age. While out on an escape, I received a juvenile sentence from the Federal System and was sent to one of the most violent Federal Prisons in the United States. I was forced to defend myself, and have been stabbed several times over the years and almost lost my life.

I would like it to be noted that no inmate can go to USP Marion unless he is in good health. After arriving at Marion, and now being here at a State Prison, it has been noted in my health records that I have developed a chronic liver disease. My wife and I are very concerned, as I have not yet received any medical check-up. I have been here for five years and have not once received any type of medical attention. I believe it's just another attempt by the State and Federal system to kill me, and who I believe are responsible for giving me my liver disease.

I have escaped numerous times in order to protect myself from the system and inmates who have tried to murder me. I have been in 34 different prisons in the United States, and so many jails that I have lost count. Why would one child, and now adult, be forced to be in so many different institutions at only 48 years of age?

I have now been sent to a state prison under the inter state compact from the state of another system. I'm finishing a 7-year sentence that was bumped up to 30-years because of my escapes. I started this sentence in 1983, and at this time, I have 17 years served on it. I also have a federal sentence that I have yet to serve for trying to use the courts in order to escape again.

I was just denied parole to my Federal sentence by the State and was told that I have to serve the rest of my time, which is 4 years and 10-months, before I can start my Federal sentence. By then I will have served approximately 28 years. I haven't been given a sentence, nor committed a crime that the public would see fit that I be confined so long. Why is this so?

Amnesty International, my wife and I spent our money that we had saved in order to obtain two lawyers that we believed would help us seek my release from prison. They did nothing but take our

228

money. We filed a petition for an Executive Pardon to the President of the United States on June 30, 1999 without any response to this date.

3. HAVE YOU REPORTED THIS INCIDENT TO AUTHORITIES VIA A GRIEVANCE PROCEDURE? WHEN?

Yes, I have reported this to the authorities, and have filed many grievances. Most of them went unanswered, or I would just be moved to another solitary cell in a different prison.

4. IF YOU FILED A GRIEVANCE WHAT WAS THE OUTCOME OF THAT PROCEDURE?

I was moved to another prison, and had my life placed in danger. I have a Senator looking into this matter, but the BOP has not responded to date. The United States Attorney General has been informed, and has not responded.

5. IF YOU FILED A GRIEVANCE, WERE YOU THREATENED WITH ANY KIND OF RETALIATION FOR DOING SO? BY WHOM?

Yes, by numerous Prison and BOP officials. They placed me in danger by putting me in the same prison, rooms, and cells, with those who wished to take my life. Because of this, I have suffered injury, and was also forced to cause harm in order to save my life. It's a war zone in here, and I have been stabbed several times.

6. IS THERE SOMEONE WE CAN CONTACT ON YOUR

BEHALF (FOR EXAMPLE, A FAMILY MEMBER OR LAWYERS) WHO IS AUTHORIZED BY YOU TO ACT ON YOUR BEHALF? IF SO, PLEASE GIVE NAME, ADDRESS, PHONE OR OTHER CONTACT INFORMATION.

Yes, my wife. We have also reached out to the United States Senator, and both the President and Attorney General of the United States, begging for help.

Amnesty, would you please HELP ME and my loving wife? We ask you in God's name to please help us. Please send someone to come talk with me, and to contact my wife.

Thank you for your time and concern in this matter, and may God bless you always.

Danny Lee Amos

This plea for help went unanswered to date…

Chapter 22

Trenton, NJ

I believe it was 1996 when I was transferred out of Florence under the Interstate Compact Agreement (it allowed out-of-state prisoners to be housed for a fee) after serving several more years in solitary and according to them, in good health. Accompanied by another convict with a similar background, (the only difference between the two of us was that he was handed a 190 year sentence right from the start) we were transported under a 'high security' status via land and air and eventually turned over to the New Jersey Department of Corrections where we went our separate ways.

I was to finish my 30 year Wisconsin sentence there before being returned to the Federal system where I still had a 57 month (4 years and 9 months) bid to complete.

I was locked down in solitary for so long without any human contact that being around another human brought on an unbelievably high level of anxiety. In fact, it made me so anxious that it felt as if I were going to burst and all I wanted was to be returned to my cage. I had become a victim of relentless isolation and literally couldn't handle being around other people. Unbeknownst to me, by the time I made it to New Jersey, I was suffering from severe anxiety attacks. Although I knew what I was feeling wasn't 'normal,' I felt if anyone came too close to me I could end up harming them.

My first placement within the New Jersey prison system was at CRAF (Central Reception and Assignment Facility). I arrived while being escorted by armed guards and special ground security. Since the guards at CRAF didn't know why I was so heavily guarded, they asked me where I was coming from. I replied, "Marion," and one of them asked if that's the one that's underground.

When I said, "Yes, some of it's buried," the same guard immediately left to make a phone call. Within seconds, a Sergeant appeared and repeated the same questions. He then nodded to the property guard who stated that all I had come with was a carton of smokes and a pair of illegal tennis shoes.

Being that I had owned those sneakers for years, I asked him how they could be illegal if I had purchased them from the prison store? He went on to say that they were 'different' than the ones they sold, so I wasn't allowed to have them. Now I've only been at the reception center for a few minutes and am already mad. I told the guard that it didn't make any sense for me to throw anything away that I had paid for just because they didn't sell the same thing at this prison. I also told him that I wasn't able to buy another pair of shoes from them, and wasn't going to go without until I could. Although the Sergeant was standing right there and heard the whole thing, the property guard looked at him and said, "This inmate (that's what convicts are called in New Jersey) refuses to give up his contraband."

Looking a bit confused, the Sergeant pulled the guard aside and whispered something to him. When they returned, the property guard reluctantly gave me my carton of cigarettes and tennis shoes. The Sergeant then informed me that I would be held in a single cell until I was transferred to my 'permanent' destination. Being okay with that, I told him that I wanted access to my property, which was shipped ahead and included several boxes of legal material and law books. He told me that he would look into it and signaled to the other

232

guards to escort me to my temporary cell.

The very next morning, the cellblock guard on duty brought an inmate over to my cell and told him that he had the top bunk. I jumped up and moved quickly to the door as the inmate started to walk in. I told him that I meant no disrespect towards him, but that he couldn't bunk with me. Of course, the inmate had no idea what was going on when the guard told me that I wasn't the one running that cellblock, and that he was my new cellmate. Holding my ground I told him, "This may not be my cellblock, but no one is living in this cage with me, so call your security and report me if you want. Now get the hell away from me and leave me alone."

Totally unaccustomed to being responded to in the fashion that I did, the guard pushed the security alarm and within seconds numerous guards came running in. As soon as the Lieutenant arrived, he asked the guard what had happened. After hearing him out, he looked at me and asked, "What's the problem?"

I informed the Lieutenant that I had not had a cell mate in over 15 years, and that I wasn't gonna start sharing a cage now. With a quick nod, the Lieutenant acknowledged what I said and told the guard that he'd be back in a few minutes. He also instructed the guard to assign the inmate to a different cell. As he left, he told all the other guards who were standing around to return to their posts. In less than half an hour, the Lieutenant returned to the cellblock accompanied by both the cellblock guard, and Assistant Warden.

With a somewhat annoyed look, the Assistant Warden (a female) asked me what the problem was. I simply replied with the same answer that I had given the Lieutenant. She then said neither the cellblock guard, nor Lieutenant were aware of my situation and that they were going to honor my request for a single cell until I was transferred out. Before she had an opportunity to turn away, I told her that I also wanted access to my law books that I hadn't received yet. She quickly informed me that I would receive them that day, and that New Jersey does not cater to inmates. She also told me that if I thought I was someplace where I could demand anything, I was mistaken.

I didn't hesitate to tell her that although I meant no disrespect towards her or anyone else there, that no one should think for one minute that they could put demands on me, and that if that were the case, I would request a transfer back to Marion because I wasn't a typical New Jersey prisoner. Apparently infuriated by my defiance, she told me not to worry because I wasn't going to be there very long, and she stormed away.

The following day, I was taken to classification where I was informed that I would be transferred to the Northern State Prison in Newark, New Jersey. I asked if it was a single cell facility, and was informed that it wasn't. Shaking my head and shrugging my shoulders I said, "Look. I've been locked down in solitary for years, and I can't live in a double cell until I get comfortable with being around people again. I'm asking that you please honor my request for a single cell facility, or ship me back to Marion because that's what I'll get there."

Obviously not understanding what I was saying, I was asked why I would want to go back to being isolated when they were trying to make my life a little better. The clerk who was processing me suggested that I at least give Northern State a try, and that if I didn't like it there, I could request a transfer to either New Jersey State Prison or Rahway. Completely frustrated by the whole process, I told the clerk that he didn't understand where I was coming from. I told him that I wasn't used to the way New Jersey prisons were run, and that I needed to be in a penitentiary setting. I tried to explain that it

234

wasn't a 'normal' thing for me to be transferred out the very next day, and that the process of being transferred between facilities typically took weeks or months to complete. All of this seemed to go in one ear, and out the other. The very next day I was transferred to a prison in Kearny instead of Newark.

Chapter 23

Kearny, NJ

As soon as I stepped foot into the Kearny facility, I realized how easy it would be to get away from there. It was mind-boggling. All through processing, I just kept thinking that if I were left there long enough I would definitely find a way out.

That very same evening as I waited in my cell for rec to be called out, I heard a lot of noise and running on the tier. As I pressed my face against the bars, I could see about 20 guards racing towards my cell. Seconds later, they were all at my cell door, yelling at me to turn around and face the wall. Still absolutely clueless as to what was going on, I turned around. The guards immediately rushed in, pulled my arms behind my back, and handcuffed me. While being pulled out of the cell, I was informed that the Warden wanted to see me. *After all that drama all I could think was "Jesus Christ ... all of that because the Warden wants to see me?*

After being escorted to the Warden's office, I was told to sit down until he was ready to see me. A moment later, he came in and said, "Someone has made a huge mistake Mr. Amos, and I really don't know how you could possibly end up in my prison, but we have a van ready to take you to the maximum security building where you'll stay until you're transported to Northern State Prison."

As I was being taken through the building, I clearly heard the guards talking down to the inmates as if they were garbage. I also saw a couple of guards beating on an inmate, and the walls were full of paintings of cartoon characters beating on prisoners. The next morning when I arrived at the processing department, I told the Sergeant that this unit wasn't going to work for me and that I wanted to be returned to Marion immediately. I also told him that I wasn't going to let any of his guards beat me or stick me with a bogus charge, and that they didn't know how to deal with convicts. Taken back by my words he responded that there were no convicts there, and that I didn't have to worry about any of his guards because I would be leaving that afternoon.

Chapter 24

Newark, NJ

A few hours later I was picked up and reunited with the convict that had made the journey from Florence with me. We were taken to Northern State, and placed into separate high-security solitary cells. We had only been there a few minutes before one of the guards decided to stand outside the fence that surrounded our cells and talk smack. He started calling us names and threatening to mess us up. He told us that he was going to burn us alive in our cage and while looking at me, he told me that he had left his shoes under my mother's bed, and he wanted them back. *Boy did he make me mad! I was so angry that if I could have gotten my hands on him through the fence, that guard would have been on the floor in no time. I guess it wasn't enough for him that I was suffering from severe anxiety.*

That guard was so into his trash talking that he didn't notice when the Lieutenant walked up on him. The Lieutenant told the guard to shut the hell up, and ordered him out of the area. As the guard walked away with his tail between his legs, the Lieutenant apologized to us both. He then handed us each a pack of smokes, and told us that we would hopefully be shipped out to Trenton or Rahway later that day because the administration didn't want either one of us there.

Through the grapevine we found out that Northern State was trying to have us sent to Trenton's SMU (Special Maximum Unit). It was probably the closest thing to Marion that Jersey has, but the main office in Trenton was refusing to take us in since neither of us had done anything that would warrant our transfer there. Later that night, the convict that I had traveled so far with stabbed a guard while he was handing him his dinner tray. I watched as he was dragged from his cell, never to be seen again. The following morning I was escorted to the Property Area to meet with the Warden. I thought the whole thing was weird, even though I was in chains. Security in the main compound was fairly lax so I asked the guards if Northern State was an honor camp.

They laughed as they told me that it wasn't, and when I asked if I was going to be staying at Northern State, they quickly replied, "We sure as hell hope not!" *That was actually a bit disheartening since, once again, I was thinking of freedom.*

Upon arriving in the property area, I was taken into a small room where the Warden was waiting for me along with several other guards. He started by telling me that although he didn't want me there, he was ordered by the folks in Trenton to release me into general population. He then said, "Mr. Amos, you don't belong here and that's something that we both know. I need your word that you are not going to harm any of my staff or inmate upon entering general population."

I told him he had my word that I would not be the cause of any trouble as long as the guards and inmates kept their hands off of me. However, I can't live in a double cell.

Acknowledging my statement, he nodded and said, "I realize that Mr. Amos, a grave injustice has been committed against you and you should have been released slowly back into the prison population over time. Unfortunately, you'll essentially need to be 'reprogrammed' to socialize with other people, and we just don't have the facilities you need here."

Feeling that he was speaking sincerely, I told him that I recognized the fact that I needed to re-adjust to people, and that was something I truly wanted to do. I told him that I would try a double cell. After a moment of silence, he said, "Look. If you feel you can't handle it, or think you're about to go off the deep end, tell the guards that you need to see me. They have been instructed to call me immediately, and then we'll see about moving you to Trenton or Rahway. Alright?" With a sigh I agreed.

I was housed in a unit adjacent to the Administration building. Everyday like clockwork, the guards would cut open my mattress and search my cell for weapons. I was also searched before going anywhere, or coming back from anywhere within the unit. I was downright treated like dirt, and constantly told that I wasn't wanted or welcomed at Northern State by every guard that I had the misfortune of coming into contact with.

As if I wasn't having a hard enough time readjusting to people in gen pop and taking all the crap from the guards, the inmates were no better. They all walked around like they were killers (little did I know that when I arrived, I was actually housed within the Northern State Gang Unit, and some of them probably were killers), and liked to talk a lot of trash. One day as I was walking to get my tray in the mess hall, I noticed three guys just staring at me. Before I knew it, my old ways were back and I asked them what they were looking at. Quickly growing tired of exchanging words with them, I said, "Listen, let's just take this to the yard and deal with it like men... talk is cheap."

They quickly responded that they were going to *serve* me, which I understood to mean that they were going to stab me. We all parted ways and as soon as I got back to my housing unit I asked an old timer if he had a shank that I could use. Without hesitation he said, "Sure KC, but what's the problem?"

Not wanting to get him involved any further, I told him that there was no problem and that I just wanted to borrow it. As soon as he gave me his shank, I went straight to the yard. From a distance it was clear to see the three guys looking my way, so I walked right up to them and pulled out the shank. Almost perfectly on cue, they all jumped back in total shock saying "Yo man! What the hell are you doin'? Are you crazy?"

Now I'm the one who's wondering what the hell's going on so I said, "I thought you all said you were going to serve me?"

With a jittery smile, one of them replied, "Yeah man, but we were just talking about fighting you. Not that kind of action dog!"

Pretty upset at this point, I asked them why they would want to fight me. I started to charge towards them, and they all turned around and took off running back to their unit.

Right then and there I knew that place was full of nothing but punks with big mouths. I returned to my housing unit and thanked the old timer whose shank I had borrowed. I told him that I probably wouldn't need to borrow it again, and went to bed. The next morning while I was out in the yard, I saw the Warden walking down the sidewalk, so I called him over. When he reached the fence, I told him that I just couldn't make it in his prison, and that if he didn't transfer me out to Trenton or Rahway, one of his inmates would end up in the hospital. Without hesitation, he told me to go pack my property. In less than 20 minutes I was on my way to Rahway State Prison.

Chapter 25

Rahway, NJ

As was the norm, I arrived at Rahway and was sent straight to solitary (at Rahway it's referred to as the 'Red Top'). I guess that's because the building has a red roof. After spending my first few days locked down, I was transported to the Administration building for a meeting. During the short drive there, I noticed that Rahway was similar to most of the facilities where I had been in. It was an old prison surrounded by a wall. I was met by the Chief of Security and escorted to his office.

He offered me a pack of smokes, and informed me that he had been the Chief at Rahway for years. He also told me that he was also part American Indian, and actually had quite a bit of Indian artwork hanging in his office. He went on to say that he was housing three other convicts from Marion who seemed to being doing well there, and that he felt there was no reason why I couldn't deal with the place as well. As he continued, he told me that the prison was 'wide-open' and that was something the cons generally liked. He told me that everything I was accustomed to was available at Rahway, and that I could just about do anything I wanted there.

However, there was one thing I needed to know. He said, "KC, come over here. I wanna show you something." As I stood up, he motioned to the guards to let me walk over to him. When I got to the window where he was standing, I could clearly see the prison yard. It was rather big, all dirt, and full of convicts. He told me to look out at the yard, and guess how many convicts were out there. Then he said, "You see all those cons...well two or three out of every four belong to me."

Not really understanding what he was talking about, and based on the last time I interpreted something that someone had told me, I asked him, "What do you mean?"

He told me that two or three out of every four convicts would make sure that he knew what was going on in the prison at all times. With a smile he said, "So, you can do whatever you want to here KC, but that doesn't mean that I won't know about it!"

Being genuinely impressed by his candor, I smiled back and said, "'Okay Chief. Thanks for the heads up."

As we turned away from the window, he put his hand on my shoulder and told me that even though I was an 'old' thinking convict, and Rahway may look like all the other prisons that I'd been in, it wasn't just a place full of cons. He told me flat out that although Rahway had its share of killers and hard-core criminals, it was full of inmates who wanted favors from him. He told me that he took good care of those who kept him well informed because he needed to know what they knew. He even told me that although sometimes the information was wrong, he would just write it off as a loss because usually the information was right.

Now totally impressed by this man I said, "Damn, Chief! You really got it goin' on here."

With a big grin he said, "That's right, KC, good luck here". He then called in a Sergeant and told him to escort me to the Four Wing Cell Block, and make sure that I was assigned to a single cell.

The Sergeant walked me over to my permanent housing unit and before leaving he told the cellblock guard that the Warden wanted me assigned to a single cell.

243

Acknowledging the Sergeant's orders, the cellblock guard told the 'wing clerk' (that's another name for a prisoner who's assigned as a tier rep) to show me to my cell. The clerk checked some paperwork, rattled off the cell number to the guard, and told him that he'd be right back. As we started walking toward the cell, the guard called the clerk back and told me to wait for him where I was.

After about a minute or so, the clerk came back and showed me to my cell. It was probably the smallest cell I had ever seen, as it was literally a cage. It was constructed completely of steel, including a steel bed that hung by chains from the wall. There was also a tiny steel footlocker and a steel table, which also hung from chains on the wall. The chair, toilet, and basin were also made of steel. As the clerk opened the door, he told me that the guard had called him back to give him the run-down on me, and that he wanted him to find out where my head was at. As soon as we walked in the cell, the wing clerk asked me if I wanted to split a joint, and I gladly accepted. As we smoked and chitchatted, I thanked him for the heads up on the cellblock guard. *It seemed that the wing clerk, a young Italian fella, took an immediate liking to me. He would eventually become a part of my family through marriage.* The next day I was assigned a job where I was instructed to sweep the floors in the cellblock. The wing clerk and I quickly became friends, and I started to move about the prison meeting different inmates. I wasted no time in trying to make some money so I could get on my feet and buy the things I needed in order to adapt to life in Rahway.

I spread the word that I was an artist, and was looking for someone to front me drawing paper and colored pencils so that I could make cards to sell at $5.00 a pop.

A few days later, I ran into a couple of bikers who agreed to front me the supplies and in less than a week I had made enough money to pay them back. During my first year at Rahway, I must have made at least 500 cards. *Not bad money for doing something that I truly enjoyed.* In time, I was making enough money to become a bit of a 'pot-head'. I learned the wing clerk that I had become good friends with was also hooked on dope, so I was able to help him out with money to pay for his habit as well.

Since he was a great cook, he helped me out with food and always made sure that I had something to eat. Even though I easily became acclimated to life at Rahway, I was still missing something. As even more time passed, my Italian friend told me about his girlfriend and that she had a friend who was single. He told me that she was 23 years old, very nice, and that she wanted to meet me. Figuring that I had nothing to lose by meeting her, I put her on my visit list. I thought she was great and despite hitting it off right away, I told her from the beginning that we could never have a long lasting relationship. There was something about her however that I just couldn't figure out. She seemed determined to make my life at Rahway as bearable as possible. This was something that although I was truly grateful for, made me feel a bit uneasy. I told myself that during the next visit, I was going to ask her what the motivation behind her kindness was. As usual, we started our visit by me thanking her for everything she did for me, and then we caught each other up on what went on during our week. Before I knew it, there was only 15 minutes left before our visit was scheduled to end, so I casually asked her why she was so kind towards me. *Wow, was I in for a shocker!*

As calm as a cucumber, she told me that all she wanted from me was a baby. In absolute shock, I said, "A baby?" to which she replied with a simple, "Yes." As it turned out, making babies in

Rahway was not unusual. I had heard that many babies were born over the years from relationships there, but I still couldn't understand why a 23 year old girl would want to raise a baby on her own.

I asked her, "Why would you want a baby from me?"

"So I can collect welfare, and because I know that the baby would be beautiful and it would help me to hang on to you!" *I can honestly say that those were some of the scariest words I had ever heard.*

Shaking my head in total disbelief, I told her to leave the visit hall and to never come back. Luckily, that made her mad so she quickly left. Needless to say, I removed her from my visit list.

As time went on in Rahway I continued to settle in, and overall I could say that things were going as well as they could be considering the circumstances. Of course, some people will always go outta their way to make someone else's life miserable. One day on my way to the yard, I was stopped by a guard who informed me that he wanted to search me. He motioned to the room ahead of us, and knowing that everyone had their eye on me, I didn't think much of it. I told him "Okay" which turned out to be a big mistake on my part. As soon as I entered the room, he sucker punched me in the back of my head. As I turned towards him he said, "I hear you like to stab guards."

As he rushed towards me, I was able to get a couple of punches in before several other guards and the Chief came running in. The Chief immediately ordered everyone to stand down, and told me to follow him. As soon as we got to his office, he asked me what had happened. I quickly replied that he should ask his guard. He called the guard in, and with me standing right there, he asked him what happened. With no sense of wrongdoing, he told the Chief that he had been told that I stabbed a guard at another prison.

Sounding a bit taken back by his response, he looked at the guard and said, "Well first and foremost, he sure as hell didn't stab anyone here and second, there's always two sides to a story. As far as I'm concerned this whole thing never went down. Understand?"

Apparently annoyed by the Chiefs apathy, the guard resentfully said, "Right. It never happened."

The Chief looked at me and asked how I felt about just dropping the whole thing. Not really affected by the whole incident, I said to the Chief, "No biggie. He threw his punches and I threw mine, so we're even." Nodding in agreement, the Chief told the guard to stay put and walked me out of his office. He told me to just go on about my business as if I was never stopped.

As soon as I stepped into the yard, the guys I was going to work out with came up and asked what had happened. Being that I knew they would just go back to the Chief and tell him what I said, I told them that there was just a misunderstanding and that I didn't want to talk about it. That squashed the whole thing as far as everyone was concerned.

Chapter 26

Atlanta, GA

A few weeks later, I was picked up by the U.S. Marshalls and taken back to the Atlanta Federal Prison where I was to testify in the penalty case of a convicted guard killer. I, along with a few other convicts, witnessed a guard's murder during a prison robbery. Although our role in the trial was that of witnesses, we were originally charged with the robbery, but eventually found not guilty by the prison board. Despite our innocence however, we were all subsequently transferred out of Atlanta. *Atlanta was another extremely violent prison and throughout my stay there, I had witnessed more murders and assaults than all the other prisons combined. No one was safe, especially the guards. One specific incident involved a female guard. During her rounds, one of the convicts came up behind her and hit her over the head with a hammer. He dragged her unconscious body into the closest cell, and numerous convicts took turns raping her. By the time the guys were done with her and the other guards had found her, it was too late. She never woke up.*

During our testimony, we attempted to provide the prison board with factual evidence that the killer, who was about to be put to death, was in fact a product of the system. We even pointed out that despite the fact that the very same convict committed several other murders while incarcerated, he was never removed from general population, which allowed him the opportunity to continue killing other inmates. But of course, now that the convict had killed a guard, he's all of a sudden deemed dangerous.

Unsurprisingly, we all took beatings from the guards in Atlanta for testifying on the convict's behalf. Luckily for us, the federal judge presiding over the trial noticed that we were covered with cuts and bruises the next day. He asked us what happened, and when we told him all about the retaliatory beatings, he ordered us transferred to the county jail for our protection. During the trial, everything came to light- even how dirty the deceased guard had been. When the convict on trial was put on the stand, he didn't hold back one bit. He named countless guards on the take, including those with high ranks, and identified the guards in charge of bringing drugs. He told the judge how the dead guard was killed because he was part of the robbery and didn't live up to his part of the bargain. Needless to say, despite all the testimony against the system, the convict was found guilty, and was given the death penalty.

Chapter 27

Back to Rahway

As soon as the trial had ended, I was transferred back to Rahway. I was received by a bunch of guards who believed that I was involved in the killing of a different guard while in Atlanta. It took about a month of close calls, and finally a confirmation from Atlanta that I wasn't involved in the murder in order to set the record straight and end the harassment.

However, despite the guards finally laying off me, something within me felt uneasy. At first, I thought it was due to the beating that I had received while in Atlanta, but the feeling kept on getting worse. I got so weak that I couldn't even workout. I had a constant sharp pain under my right side rib cage, which caused me to completely lose my appetite. I started having stomach problems and quickly lost weight. On top of all that, I was constantly having upper respiratory infections. I felt like a mess, and couldn't figure out why. Throughout all of my suffering through those symptoms, I never thought back to the incident with the paperwork at Marion. Since I didn't know what Hepatitis was, and I certainly wasn't yellow, I never connected the two. Besides, Florence gave me a clean bill of health when I was there, and Rahway told me that I was so healthy that I'd live to be a 100.

It finally got to the point where I could barely stand up, so I decided to go to the hospital. After they did the blood work, the doctor came back and informed me that I was just run down, and was suffering from fatigue. He gave me some antibiotics, told me to rest, and assured me that I would be fine in a few days. Unsurprisingly I wasn't any better, so I went back to the hospital a couple of days later. *Keep in mind that every time a convict is seen by a doctor or goes to the hospital at his request, he's charged for the visit!* This time I was told that there was nothing wrong with me, and that I shouldn't drink any alcohol and make sure to practice safe sex!

That was the last straw for me. I told those people that they were complete idiots, and that they were just ripping me off. I stammered, "The only thing I drink is your water, and who the hell would I be having sex with? If you haven't noticed… I'M IN PRISON!!!"

I requested an HIV test since so many cons at Rahway were infected, and neither I, nor the idiots working in the medical unit could figure out what was wrong with me. I wanted to eliminate that as a possibility. They took the blood samples, and told me they'd call me back to go over the results in 2 weeks. One week later, I was called back to the hospital and I immediately started to panic. When they tell you '2 weeks', that usually means a minimum of two weeks, so for them to be calling me back sooner is definitely a reason for concern. I was in a state of panic the entire way to the hospital. All I kept thinking was, 'Oh my God, I've got HIV.'

When I finally got to the hospital, I was greeted by the one nurse who hated me. You could see the hatred in her face because last time I was there I kept insisting that there was something wrong with me, and that they were too stupid to figure it out. *She worked for CMS (Correctional Medical Services). A company contracted by the state to provide cheap, substandard services to convicts which would eventually help kill them off.* As soon as she saw me, she smiled and said, "Mr. Amos, how do you think your tests came back?" I told her that I hoped they were negative. Still smiling, she shook her head and said, "Well I'm sorry, but they came back positive. Please come into my office."

I was in total shock by what I was just told, and I literally fell into the chair in her office. She told me that I would have to start HIV treatment, and that the doctor would explain the process to me. She also said that my liver tests came back a little high, so I would need antibiotics for that. She was talking to me as if all I had was a mere cold.

Devastated by the news, I asked her, "How long do I have to live?" She cheerfully replied, "I don't know Mr. Amos. I'm not God, you know. Just go have a seat outside and wait for the doctor to call you." *I swear all I wanted to do was get up and bite her nose off to take that smug look off of her face.*

As I waited for the doctor, I started thinking about all those beatings and fights that I had been in where blood was drawn from all sides. I thought to myself that I should go back to my cellblock, tape a shank to my hands, and take out all the guards and convicts that had wronged me. I was determined not to go out alone. Although I saw the doctor come out and could hear him calling to me, my legs just wouldn't move. Since I was the only one sitting in the waiting room, he called out to me a couple of more times before going back into the nurse's office. A few seconds later, both the doctor and the nurse came out where she pointed to me and said, "There he is."

I looked at both of them and said, "Wait a minute, my name is Amos."

Immediately, she said, "'Oh my God, I must have gotten the medical records mixed up, but you still need to see the doctor for the antibiotics."

I was furious. I told her that she was the stupidest person that I had ever met, and that what she had just done was the cruelest thing that could ever be done to anyone. I also told her that she had essentially given me a death sentence, and taken it back in less than ten minutes. That miserable woman just smiled and walked away.

The doctor put his hand on my shoulder, and asked me to come into his office. As soon as he closed the door he shook his head and told me that it was hard to find good help. We sat down and he opened my file on his desk. Despite the sticker that read 'Hepatitis' in the file, he told me that I was in good health but had an upper respiratory infection and that the antibiotics would help.

I left the doctor's office the same way I went in - totally clueless as to what was really wrong with me. Seeing that sticker reminded me of what the con at Marion had showed me, so through the FOIA, I requested a copy of my medical records which included the last test results which the incompetent nurse had lied to me about. When I received my file, I found that it clearly said that the hepatitis test had been performed incorrectly, and needed to be resubmitted because the blood sample provided was clotted. That proved that the CMS nurse purposely lied about the results, and was retaliating against me for trying to seek help.

Soon afterwards, I was transferred to Riverfront State Prison in Camden, NJ. My health continued to deteriorate there. My weight dropped another twenty pounds, my muscles and joints ached constantly, and I always had the chills. I also suffered from cold sweats, dizziness, headaches and fever. Again I sought medical attention, but to no avail. Unfortunately, Riverfront also contracted CMS to handle their medical program, so I heard the exact same response. "There's nothing wrong with you Mr. Amos. You just need to stay away from drinking any alcohol, and make sure to practice safe sex." Fed up by the lack of medical assistance I was receiving, I started writing everybody that I could think of that might be able to help me find out why I was so sick.

My luck finally changed when I wrote the Philadelphia Inquirer. They took an interest in my plight, and sent a reporter to visit and interview me. He was able to take a copy of my lab work back with him, and got it in the hands of a liver specialist who worked at UMDNJ (University of Medicine and Dentistry of New Jersey) in Newark. Just as I had suspected, there was indeed something wrong with me. The liver specialist told the reporter that although I didn't have HIV, I was in fact dying. He confirmed what the paper I saw at Marion stated. I had chronic Hepatitis B & C, and it was getting worse by the day. The specialist told the reporter that it was so advanced that if I didn't get help immediately, I would soon be dead. Thanks to that reporter, whom I consider a dear friend for publishing my situation and bringing it to light, I'm alive today.

As soon as the Department of Corrections got wind of what was going on, they started threatening to lock me down. According to them, I had just opened a can of worms. Despite knowing the gravity of my situation, they continued to deny me treatment. They insisted that the cost for treatment was too high and that since my case was so advanced, it would just be a waste of government money. Eventually my persistence to live prevailed, and I was granted the treatment I deserved. The treatment itself was horrendous but I knew it was the *only* alternative to death. It consisted of 48 weeks of medication and injections in my belly and legs. That was probably the worst time of my life, but I suffered through it by thinking of all those convicts who had essentially been murdered by the prison system by allowing them to get sick, and then denying them their treatment. *I guess that's the 'express' form of capital punishment - without the appeals process.*

The harassment continued as the prison and medical services staff collaborated to try and end my treatment. Guards continued to assault me, the medical staff improperly administered my shots, and the administration threatened me numerous times since I had sought outside help on my behalf. Nonetheless, I survived. As odd as it may seem, my ordeal actually helped other convicts to obtain future treatments, and a specialized unit for convicts with Hepatitis and HIV exists in numerous prisons today.

There is currently a Class Action Lawsuit in the federal court against the Department of Corrections for their willful neglect of those convicts who contracted Hepatitis while imprisoned.

Soon after my treatment was complete, I was transferred to South Wood Prison in Bridgeton, NJ where my life remained in danger. I was repeatedly threatened with death by the guards, and my property was destroyed - including all of my post-treatment medications. It was at South Wood that I was diagnosed with PTSD (Post Traumatic Stress Disorder) as a result from psychological and physical abuse endured during my Hepatitis treatment.

Chapter 28

Emancipation

With that whole ordeal finally behind me, I can reminisce about my life and come to terms with the fact that this entire crazy journey was put into motion on the day my mother chose to relinquish her parental rights. The only valid crime that I had personally committed against society was to steal as a juvenile. I remain caged within a human warehouse almost 50 years later as a result of my crimes that I have committed within the *system* that were necessary for me to be alive today.

I've been institutionalized in a total of 34 facilities, some of which include:

Federal Prisons - El Reno, Ashland, Petersburg, Memphis, Terre Haute, Leavenworth, Sandstone, USP Lompoc, Lewisburg, McNeil Island, USP Marion (super max facility), ADX Florence (super max facility), Atlanta, Oxford, Springfield, U.S.P Camdan, FCI Talladega

State Penitentiaries - Missouri, Stillwater, Waupun, Green Bay, Dodge, Portage (named Columbia Correctional), Fox Lake, Kettle Moraine, and Rahway

State Prisons - Riverfront, South Woods, and CRAF

Youth Detention Centers - McCune, Algoa, and Boonville

I'm ecstatic to say that the chapter has 'officially' closed on all state sentences! I have served time in several states for 'escape' related charges, with my last bid being in Wisconsin where I was originally sentenced to serve 7 years. Incredibly, that sentence escalated into 30 years.

Believe it or not, murderers typically serve that amount of time. I watched countless murderers come to prison and serve less time than what I was doing. I'd see them serve their time, be released, and return again from committing new crimes while I remained in prison to serve my time for the internally added charges.

Again, I've come to the conclusion that all of that is behind me now because there is nothing I can do to change that part of my life. I finished this book as I was serving the last of my sentence for one last attempted escape to be free. Despite my good conduct since then, I haven't received any good behavior reprieve. What I have received is a Male Custody Classification Profile Form, which means that even after all of my years of good conduct, I'm viewed on the Public Safety Factor scale as 'Greatest Risk'. This profile is sent to the Parole Agent, the House Officials, and anyone that would be looking at giving me a chance to become successful upon my return to society. This 'greatest risk' label given to me means that I'm a severe risk to the public because of the crimes that I've committed over the past 40 years, while in prison. In case this didn't turn society against me, they also noted that I am a serious risk for violence. I feel like I've paid my debt to the system, and to those who I've wronged while I was serving my time.

I questioned why this was all being written against me when I hadn't tried escaping in several years, I hadn't been involved in violence of any type in several years, I hadn't committed any crimes in several years, and I hadn't even been involved with the public in decades. The answer to my question was simply "You'll always be viewed as such, and there's nothing you can do about it." After hearing that, I knew that I would be doomed as soon as I walked through the door to freedom unless I stayed strong and kept a positive attitude.

I know one thing for sure, and that is that I am one year away from finishing my federal sentence. After that, I will have a supervised release by state and federal parole agents until the year 2022. I remember submitting a formal request to my unit team who are assigned to assist prisoners in the cellblock with any and all issues of concern while confined here at the Federal Prison in Talladega. I thought at first that maybe it would be best for me to request to return to my home state, and live with my surviving sister until I adjusted to the changes of today's society. Once I was able to get on my feet, my plan was to then return to New Jersey to live with my loving wife. Unfortunately, the Kansas City parole agent found reason to deny my request to live with my sister. However, the agent did say that he would consider my request to have a 'halfway house' in Kansas City, which would provide me with the opportunity to find work and adjust to my new life. The only thing that was needed in order for this to happen was for my unit team to give him a call to talk through the process. The agent waited several months for the call, but no call was ever made. Every time I asked my team to help me out and make the call, they always stated they were too busy, or that they would get to it eventually. I guess the Kansas City agent felt that I must have been a bad omen because he denied my request entirely to return to my home state for any reason. I can't help but to remind you here in my book, that these government prison officials are paid good money to do their jobs, and that their wages came out of your pocket. You to be the judge; do you think they really earn it?

I've seen first-hand countless prison officials sitting for hours playing games on their computers that your tax dollars have bought.

The system in itself is not fair. Society must understand that the prison system is a money-making business, and that the prisoners (no matter what age or gender) have become a sales pitch in order to open up more prisons. It is nothing more than human slavery, and your tax dollars are being used to build more prisons. That money could be of much better use assisting those who are confined to learn how to become a productive member of society upon release. Prisoners who are released without gaining any 'real world' knowledge while incarcerated have the potential to become a serious public safety factor. No one wants to hire an ex-convict, and unfortunately, they are sometimes left with no choice but to revert back to their old ways in order to survive. The *system* knows that they are going to be back since 77% of prisoners that are released are arrested again within 5 years[1]. I can't help but think that the prison system wants them to come back so that their business will never end. I feel I would have been exposed to more opportunities to better myself over the past 50 years if they DIDN'T want me to come back. It doesn't take a rocket scientist to see that prisoners are being manipulated by certain state and federal prison officials as well. I want to say that not all prison officials have the same state of mind, but if they don't fall in line and get with the 'program', then they are out of a job.

I could go on and on about the injustices brought upon society by their wasted tax dollars going towards the prison system, but I'll wait and hope my book will bring forth the opportunity to speak upon my freedom in 2015.

Since I was denied to go to my home state, I again submitted a request to be released in New Jersey with my wife, but was informed that I would have to go to the state of Wisconsin where my last crime was committed several years ago. I wondered, 'Why would I be sent to a state where I don't know anyone when I have a loving wife who wants me to come home to her?' I couldn't help but realize that they were setting me up for failure by placing me in an unknown area where the *system* is waiting for any small opportunity to return me to prison. I decided that I had to go above the unit team's head, and explain the serious situation I was being forced into. By doing so, I was threatened by the very people whose job it is to help me with these exact issues. They told me that if I continued to seek outside help, I would suffer the consequences.

I thought long and hard about my options. I remembered that I needed to wait, and pray to God and see which door He would open for me. I have known for some years now that by placing my faith in God's will, he would lead me in the right direction and put me exactly where I needed to be. Nonetheless, I couldn't help but feel a little hopeless. I started to get angry at the devilish attempts by the system to cause me pain and suffering even as a free man, but I knew that this was the Devil's way of working on my mind. I needed to remain patient.

Some time later, a well-respected prison official arrived here in Talladega. This official and I have had a lot of history together over the past several years, and he had always been a big positive factor in my prison life. He has always been fighting wars on his side, just like I have been on mine, and I respected him for that. We both have been in some of the worst prisons in the United States, and being that we were on opposite sides, I've always held the utmost respect for him. He has always been fair to all parties involved, and no matter what else he had going on when a situation called for his attention, he refused to allow guards to beat prisoners once they were down. He always acted professionally, and if he told you he would do something, you could count on his word that he would get it done. At the same time, there was another side of him that only a fellow survivor would be able to notice. I could tell that he has had his fair share of tough 'battles' and similar to myself when faced with a life or death situation, he understood that you better be ready to fight when the time called. When it seemed like I couldn't facilitate my successful return to society, this man once again maneuvered a tactical strategy that caused myself and other prison officials to do the right thing. He acted on my behalf, and against the team's will, to set me up for success. After he had sat down with several members of my team, they decided to honor his maneuver. They were made to believe that his was the best solution for everyone involved. The result was that I would be to transferred to yet another prison so they could be finished with me and be out of their hair. This also caused them to believe that they in fact accomplished their goal of not helping me in any way. This solution helped me because I would not be a target for retaliation against me for making them do their jobs, and I was now pending a transfer to a federal prison in New Jersey where I'll be close to my loving wife and where I'll be assisted with my 2015 release. It was a win-win situation, and I owe him thanks once again. Like several times before, he had turned a negative situation into a positive one while fooling the administration into believing that they had actually accomplished their evil motives towards me. I've addressed this man in my book because I believe that God placed him in my life for a reason. I also want to express that I've found over the years that not all prison officials are terrible people. There are some who are worthy in their attempt to help prisoners in this line of work, and I've met several of them here at the end of my time.

I have also learned that I will always have the memories of those convicts whom I celled with for so many years. Some of the memories are good, some are bad, but they all have become a part of my personal life. I will forever hold these memories, and I wish them well and truly hope that my book will bring them some sort of relief. For all of those who told me that they just *couldn't figure me out*, I hope that they read this book and learn all that there is to know about me.

I cannot leave the most important factor of my life, other than God, outside of my book. If it were not for my loving wife who I married in Rahway State Prison several years ago, I'm not sure that this book would have been possible, or that I'd be where I am today. We were introduced through a friend at Rahway, and I remember the first time I saw this beautiful woman coming through the prison doors. I felt something that I had never felt before. She has brought me to life, and has stood by me with a loving and caring heart. She is the one who is responsible for bringing me to the Lord, and there is nothing more important to me in this world than that. I believe that God placed us together for a reason, and that reason is now clear. Unfortunately, I was subsequently transferred to the state of Wisconsin where I will serve the remainder of my sentence. My wife and I are now divorced, and she has since remarried and is moving on with her life like I am.

I was officially released from prison on August 11th, 2015. God is good! Since my release, I have been blessed by so many wonderful people. I had no idea that there was so much love and concern in the world. I have seen first-hand that people really do care about me, and have helped me with my transition back into society. It has not been easy after spending 50 years in prison, but I have learned that if you really want to live a crime-free life out in the real world, you can do it. It comes down to making the right decisions, and if I can do it, so can you! My story is a true testament that God moves in mysterious ways. In saying that, I truly believe that God placed me into the hands of the Balsam Lake, WI agents, and into the hands of all people in this area who have become my new family!

Everyone who has helped me since my release has been such a blessing in my new life. My agents, and those alike, have been such positive factors in helping me learn the ways of the 'real world'. The most important lesson that I have learned is that there is life after prison after all. I now work with ex-cons, and I hope that they can see me as an example of moving forward and living a life after prison. I hope they see that you CAN move forward and put everything behind you if you want it bad enough.

In ending this book, I cannot express enough how grateful I am to all of those who have stood by my side since my release. And to what family I have left, all of you are a blessing from GOD, and I love you all.

Chapter 29

My Journey

Nowadays I find myself waking up in a cold sweat and not being able to sleep because of my haunting memories. I realize that everyone in my past is slowly being carved out of my life by the invisible hand of time. I remember in my younger years calling out to God, not knowing if he was listening or even really existed, hoping that just maybe he could put an end to the abuse and stop my pain and suffering. But for whatever reason, it seemed that I could never get his attention. As time passed, I began to believe that I must have done something terribly wrong that I couldn't remember because of all the blows I had sustained to my head as a child, or that God was just too busy to come to my aid and didn't want anything to do with me. I became so angry with God that I would call him names and throw the Bible about in fits of rage, especially while in solitary. I just couldn't figure out why God, who I had been taught was the almighty and could do anything, would allow a child to suffer like I had for so many years. I kept wondering why God wouldn't stop those who inflicted so much pain and suffering on so many others under the guise of the *system*. I also kept asking myself why am I still thinking about God? After all, he has never answered any of my cries for help. But then I would just say to myself, "Well, maybe some day He'll speak to me and tell me what I did wrong." Feeling totally abandoned, I thought to myself that I would never get any where in my life unless I started using the tools that God had given me on this journey. I needed to start using my mind to try and figure out the answers to all my questions about why I was destined to this life. I had to use my sixth sense, so to speak, so that I could accomplish my mission and fulfill the reason for my existence on this earth. I reference God because there is no human who has the power to truly walk another through the pits of hell, and still inspire a sense of hope where although you're walking blind into the darkness, good things are yet to come. It was that unknown force that pushed me forward into the next day. At one time in my life I truly doubted the existence of God, but I've come to realize that it is because of His divine power that I have been able to endure this life that I have been forced into. Only God is able to protect me from the evil that lurks within these prison walls so that I can continue with the journey that I was born to make. Although I have no real understanding of the pros and cons of my journey, I have learned not to question "why", but instead accept that my life rests in God's hands. He is driving the car. Understanding that there is a purpose for my being in this earth has enabled me to realize that I am not going crazy, but instead accept that there are good things in store for me further on down the path that I'm on. Time has taught me that God works in mysterious ways. Only he knows the master plan for each of us and we can't arbitrarily change the direction of His goals.

While I know firsthand that no evil ever brought about any good, in fact it usually brings out the worst, my faith always seems to bloom in my darkest hours. Faith gives me the strength that I need to survive, and I understand that only through His divine power can wonderful things happen in my life.

In ending this book, I don't want anyone to think that the purpose of this book is to convince people to follow God, or convert to Christianity. This book is not meant to be about God. I wrote this book to help provide insight on what really takes place behind those prison walls, and the injustices that I suffered at the hands of the prison system. I mention God because He was a big part of my journey, and I truly hope that something in my book will help you through your own personal journey.

The End
Danny Lee Amos
Child 6150

Thanks to everyone who assisted me with this book, I can't thank you enough for everything.

269

An Example Of A "Development Plan"

INMATE SKILLS DEVELOPMENT PLAN

Name: AMOS, DANNY

PROGRAM REVIEW: 06-05-2013

RegNo: 35782-115

COGNITIVE

CRIMINAL BEHAVIOR
- evidence of a high risk offender
- onset of criminal behavior before the age of 14
- criminal versatility: convictions in 3 or more categories
- significant history of violence: 2 or more violent convictions

Progress and Goals

Previous TEAM 01-31-2013

Has had clear conduct as recommended. Continue this goals through next review.

Current TEAM

Inmate Amos arrived at BUT on 05/14/2013.

Unit Team has no recommendations at this time. Clear conduct since 2006

CHARACTER

Status — **Response Summary**

PERSONAL CHARACTER
- no history of behaviors indicative of positive personal character
- religious assignment: AMER IND
- no evidence easily influenced by other

PERSONAL RESPONSIBILITY
- reports responsibility for current incarceration as:
- negative life events
- no efforts to make amends for their crime(s)

Progress and Goals

Previous TEAM 01-31-2013

Contract changed from Unicor to Quarterly

Current TEAM

Inmate Amos arrived at BUT on 05/14/2013.

Unit Team recommends you continue to maintain a positive attitude and positive interactions with staff and inmate peers daily through 12/03/2013.

LEISURE

Status — **Response Summary**

USE OF LEISURE TIME
- activities indicative of positive use of leisure time;
- family time
- movies/television/music
- reading
- hobbies (includes hunting, fishing, etc.)
- library

Generated: 06-05-2013 13:32:08   Page 11   Inmate Copy ISDS Version: 1.6.1a

271

LEISURE

Progress and Goals
Previous TEAM 01-31-2013 No goals in this area **Current TEAM** Inmate Amos arrived at BUT on 05/14/2013. Unit Team recommends you participate in positive leisure activities at least three times/week through 12/03/2013. Religious activities, recreation, walking, reading, hobby craft, etc.

DAILY LIVING

Status	Response Summary
ⓘ	**FINANCIAL MANAGEMENT** ⊕ knowledge in maintaining checking account ⊕ knowledge in maintaining savings account ⊕ knowledge in utilizing an ATM debit card ⊕ knowledge in obtaining loans ⊖ no positive credit history ⊕ lived within financial means ⊖ pays monthly bills on time
✓	**FOOD MANAGEMENT** ⊕ possesses grocery shopping/consumer skills ⊕ makes good nutritional choices to maintain health ⊕ possesses basic food preparation skills ⊕ knowledgeable in accessing community resources to obtain food
✓	**PERSONAL HYGIENE/SANITATION** ⊕ good personal hygiene and sanitation ⓘ quarters assignment: HOUSE G/RANGE 08/BED 004L
ⓘ	**TRANSPORTATION** ⊖ does not have valid driver's license ⊕ No outstanding motor vehicle violations ⊖ does not own personal vehicle with appropriate insurance ⊕ possesses public transportation skills and has access to public transportation
ⓘ	**IDENTIFICATION** ⊖ does not have photo identification ⊖ does not have birth certificate ⊖ does not have social security card
ⓘ	**HOUSING** ⊖ no established housing year prior to incarceration ⊖ history of unstable housing (multiple addresses) ⊕ housing upon release ⓘ supervision district is a relocation ⓘ anticipated housing plan NOT approved by USPO(s)

272

DAILY LIVING

	① other: Has been in custody for a beter part of 50 years
?	**RESIDENTIAL REENTRY CENTER (RRC) PLACEMENT**
	① recommended or ordered for RRC placement
✓	**FAMILY CARE**
	⊕ not responsible for obtaining child care for any dependent children upon release
	⊕ not responsible for obtaining elder care for any dependent(s) upon release
	⊕ not responsible for obtaining any other special services for dependents upon release

Progress and Goals

Previous TEAM 01-31-2013

Still need release address. Submit by 06-2013

Current TEAM

Inmate Amos arrived at BUT on 05/14/2013.

FRP Part-Unit Team recommends you make FRP payments per contract until paid in full and make payments on time through 12/03/2013.

Unit Team recommends you maintain good personal hygiene and room sanitation daily through 12/03/2013.

273

INMATE SKILLS STATUS

Status	Initial Assessment 08-09-2012	Previous Assessment 01-31-2013	Current Assessment 06-05-2013
Attention Required	50%	51.1%	51.7%
Mitigating Issues	0%	0%	0%
Unanswered	20.6%	12.2%	1.1%
Satisfactory	26.1%	31.7%	42.2%
Not Applicable	3.3%	5%	5%

Skill Area	Attention Required	Mitigating Issues	Unanswered	Satisfactory	Not Applicable
Academic	5%	0%	0%	95%	0%
Vocational/Career	100%	0%	0%	0%	0%
Interpersonal	65%	0%	0%	25%	10%
Wellness	65%	0%	0%	15%	20%
Mental Health	10%	0%	0%	75%	15%
Cognitive	80%	0%	0%	20%	0%
Character	80%	0%	0%	20%	0%
Leisure	0%	0%	0%	100%	0%
Daily Living	60%	0%	10%	30%	0%

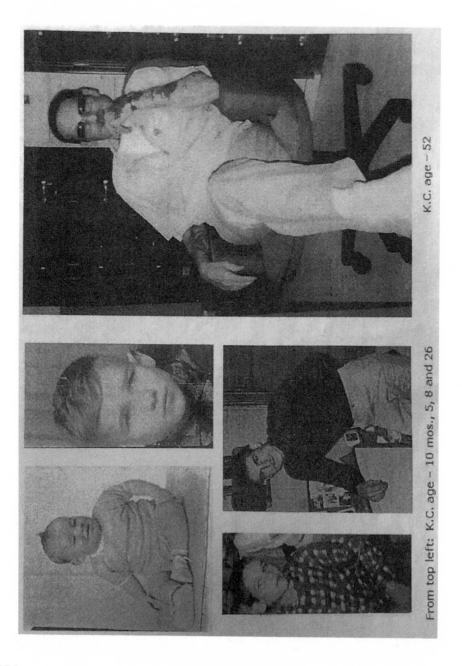

From top left: K.C. age – 10 mos., 5, 8 and 26

K.C. age – 52

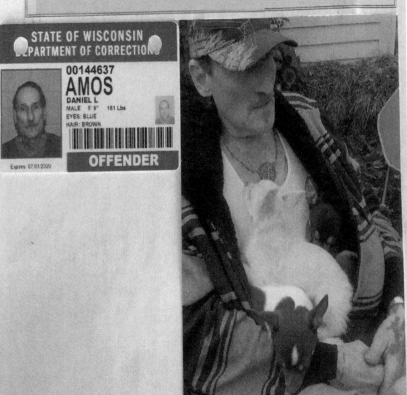

Danny is being held by his Mother

CHILD 6150

1. Statistics, Bureau of Justice. "3 In 4 Former Prisoners in 30 States Arrested Within 5 Years of Release." PR Newswire: News Distribution, Targeting and Monitoring, 22 Apr. 2014, www.prnewswire.com/news-releases/3-in-4-former-prisoners-in-30-states-arrested-within-5-years-of-release-256173261.html.

Made in the USA
Lexington, KY
25 July 2018